Building
Trust

God, Our Father and Role Model

Nancy C. Gaughan

WESTBOW
PRESS
A DIVISION OF THOMAS NELSON
& ZONDERVAN

Scripture quotations taken from the New American Standard Bible®,
Copyright © 1960, 1962, 1963, 1968, 1971, 1972, 1973, 1975, 1977, 1995
by The Lockman Foundation. Used by permission. (www.Lockman.org)

WestBow Press books may be ordered through booksellers or by contacting:

WestBow Press
A Division of Thomas Nelson & Zondervan
1663 Liberty Drive
Bloomington, IN 47403
www.westbowpress.com
1 (866) 928-1240

Because of the dynamic nature of the Internet, any web addresses or
links contained in this book may have changed since publication and
may no longer be valid. The views expressed in this work are solely those
of the author and do not necessarily reflect the views of the publisher,
and the publisher hereby disclaims any responsibility for them.

Any people depicted in stock imagery provided by Thinkstock are models,
and such images are being used for illustrative purposes only.
Certain stock imagery © Thinkstock.

ISBN: 978-1-4908-5447-2 (sc)
ISBN: 978-1-4908-5448-9 (hc)
ISBN: 978-1-4908-5446-5 (e)

Library of Congress Control Number: 2014917782

Printed in the United States of America.

WestBow Press rev. date: 10/21/2014

CONTENTS

Chapter 1   Building Trust 1

Chapter 2   In His Image.. 7

Chapter 3   We are Not God 11

Chapter 4   His Character We Strive For 20

Chapter 5   The Hats Our Father Wears 27

Chapter 6   Unconditional Love 34

Chapter 7   Unselfish Love 42

Chapter 8   Providing for Needs 49

Chapter 9   Accounting for Limitations 57

Chapter 10   Communicating Instructions and Consequences ... 66

Chapter 11   Allowing Freedom of Choice 71

Chapter 12   Keeping Your Word 78

Chapter 13   Staying in Control 85

Chapter 14   God, The Perfect Parent.. 95

Study Page 101

Scriptural References... 127

CHAPTER 1

Building Trust

Proverbs 22:6 Train a child in the way she should do and when he is old he will not turn from it.

Not only did Jesus refer to God as His Father over and over, anywhere from 40 to 50 times, depending on the translations, He referred to God as our Father anywhere from 20 to 30 times, depending on the translation. Yet, few of us have thought about God as our Father and a role model for parenting.

When it comes to our parenting, learning from our own parents' example can be a terrible handicap, for none of us had perfect parents. Some had unspeakably bad parents. While we can look to our parents to see what they did right and wrong in raising us, we have a far better role model in God, our perfect Father. In this chapter and throughout the book, we will see how our Father has built in us the confidence and given us the strength and guidance to live in the world but not become corrupted by it.

As God's children, we gain confidence and strength when we trust and obey God. Most people know the hymn, "Trust and Obey". It is important that the trust comes first. It is the foundation upon which all behavior and attitudes grow. This book is about learning to trust our Father and teaching our children to trust us,

1

their parents whom they can see, and God, their Father whom they cannot not see but is as real and an even better parent than we are.

That is the ultimate goal, to train our children to trust God, to trust and obey. There are those who sing, "Trust and Obey," but only hear the "Obey" when it comes to their children and their parenting. That is because we can require obedience of our children without developing trust.

As parents, the question is, "How are we to follow Proverb 22:6 and "train our children in the way they should go?" How do we begin to prepare our children to live in an evil world and to trust and obey God? We, of course, need to talk to them and warn them about the world, but children are notorious for not listening to or believing their parents. "That was you, this is me." "That was back in the dark ages." "You always worry." People, especially children, learn from imitation and example even more than by lecture or reading.

Our sons were Boy Scouts. Every week they recited an oath in which they pledged on their honor to do their best to do their duty to God and their country, to help other people at all times, and to keep themselves physically strong, mentally awake and morally straight. It is a code all parents should teach their children to live by. No one forced them to be Boy Scouts and recite this promise, so it was their choice and their commitment. It is a promise that was and will be difficult to live day by day all their lives because every day they will be faced with choices which the world will test. At the very outset, the world mocks this pledge.

For example, part of the pledge is to be morally straight. In 2013 our judiciary struck down several state's laws that defined marriage as between one man and one woman. They required the states to issue marriage licenses for homosexual couples. The news stories came complete with pictures of two men kissing. That we even had to try, but then could not pass a constitutional amendment to define marriage as between one male and one female and the change in Boy Scout policy to admit openly homosexual boys shows that the definition of morally straight has changed in this country. To the country at large being morally straight no longer refers to how we conduct our sexual lives.

When he was in middle school, our younger son was dismayed that most of his male classmates saw nothing wrong with premarital sex and intended to have sex by the time they were out of high school. In the school yard there seems to be little honor in the world at large. Yet, our sons and their fellow scouts from every age stand firm on their honor that they will do their best to do all the things in this pledge, including be morally straight.

The issue of being morally straight is only one difficulty a young person will have with keeping this promise. The promise is to try to do his duty to God and his country. A duty is an obligation. Those who recite this are stating they realize they have an obligation to God and to their country. Most of our country laughs at the concept of feeling one has a duty to God and country. A generally accepted statistic is that eighty to ninety percent of the work in a church is done by ten to twenty percent of the people. Where is our duty to God? If our youth all had a sense of duty to country, we would not have three of the branches of our volunteer military seriously understaffed, as they were for several years until the government decided we did not need a large military to keep us safe. A neighbor boy frequently said about his parents, "They owe me." That sentiment is the opposite of having a sense of duty and responsibility, which says, "I owe them." In 1961 Present Kennedy told the country during his inaugural address, "Ask not what your country can do for you. Ask what you can do for your country." It is a foreign concept in today's world.

Beyond battling outside opinion, it is contrary to our nature to always be helping other people. It is impossible to <u>always</u> do one's best. And from the world's point of view, mental and physical successes are to be for self-gratification and reward, not for honoring God and country. So to encourage and help our children live by this code, we must teach them to be able to stand against popular opinion and to live lives that reflect this pledge.

As parents we want our children to make Godly choices, to have the courage to live in the world and not be corrupted or beaten by it. It takes tremendous confidence to be able to face a braggart who is surrounded by adoring classmates and say, "That's not right." or stand in a crowd of classmates talking about an R rated movie and say, "I won't watch that" or to answer "Because it isn't right" when questioned why he or she doesn't do or think a great many other things the world condones. In short, it is difficult to live a life of honor.

There are those who argue we need to shield our children from the many immoral pressures they are bound to encounter in the world. But we cannot shield them forever. Eventually they will be out in the world, and they must be prepared for it. We, their parents, must prepare them. Even as we would not think of sending our military to war without training, we must prepare our children for the temptations that will surround them. As they grow up, they will be tempted to cheat and lie and become self indulgent, selfish and proud. Every day living is a battle between good and evil, as Paul explained to the Ephesians, "For our struggle is not against flesh and blood, but against the rulers, against the authorities, against the powers of this dark world and against the spiritual forces of evil in the heavenly realms." (Eph. 6:12)

Although as children we hated to hear it, as adults we still sometimes say, "Because I said so!" When that is the answer we give, we are really saying, "I want obedience whether you trust me or not." A better response, although it takes more time is, "I can't give you the answer right now; but if you trust me, you know I wouldn't ask you to do this if I didn't think it was important."

Obedience without trust is based on fear and breeds resentment. While we are told throughout the Bible to fear the Lord, obedience based on trust is wholly different than obedience based on fear without trust. The Hebrew word for fear in the bible is the same word for "revere" or "stand in awe of". When we contemplate the power and love of God and His righteousness, we should be humbled and awed and even afraid.

But it is not out of fear that He wants us to behave. We are to obey because we love Him and trust that He always has our best at heart. He tells us throughout the Bible what He wants of us and that all of His commandments are for our own good. Moses wrote in Deuteronomy 10:12-13, "And now, O Israel, what does the Lord your God ask of you but to fear (revere) the Lord your God, to walk in all his ways, to love him, to serve the Lord your God with all your heart and with all your soul, and to observe the Lord's commands and decrees that I am giving you today <u>for your own good</u>?"

Paul said in 1Cor. 7:35: "I am saying this for your own good, not to restrict you, but that you may live in a right way in undivided devotion to the Lord." And Jesus said that the obedience must be based on love and trust. "If you love me, you will obey what I command." (Jn. 14:15)

When we trust, the desire to please and to obey flows as an outgrowth of that love and trust. Trusting God and trusting us, their parents, shapes our children's behavior and attitudes. For example, trusting that the rules are for our own good, we do what we are commanded with gladness, even when it is difficult or unpleasant or when we cannot see the good.

As adults, when we tithe, or forgive someone who has hurt us, or refrain from immorality or prideful boasting or gossip, we often cannot see the good it does for us. Yet, over time we will see that the more we obey God, the more the rules are for our own good. We feel the freedom from the oppression of anger when we forgive. When we are tempted by immorality or boasting or so many other sins the world condones, we feel the strength of the Holy Spirit helping us turn away and take joy in knowing He is within us. When we trust and obey Him, we feel closer to God and our faith and conviction is strengthened.

If we trust that God loves us, we do not rebel against the rules and do not resent the punishments when we fail, repent and confess.

5

We know, as Solomon said, "The Lord disciplines those he loves, as a father the son he delights in." (Prov. 3:12) We accept God's discipline as the Holy Spirit reveals our sin to us.

This trust also affects our attitudes. Having the bible to show us God's promises and direction for us, we can go through life with confidence. The confidence comes in knowing we always have God to turn to and that help is always at hand. We develop this trust by learning and believing God is who He says He is in the bible and that He can and will do all He has promised. In short, our confidence comes because of who God is, not because of who we are. We have no merit on our own apart from the sacrifice Jesus made for us. So while we are learning to trust God, we are also learning humility. As God's character has inspired our faith and trust in Him, so must our character inspire our children's faith and trust.

Trust is neither deserved nor owed. It is earned. Just as God has earned our trust, we can earn the trust of our children. We can teach them to trust us, their parents, and trust God their Father. God has given us our children to show them what He is like. (Prov. 22:6) So we look to how He has developed that trust in us, to see how He can help us and to see how we can imitate Him in our own parenting. The goal of this book is twofold, to help the reader better understand God, our Father, and his/her relationship with Him, and to use that understanding to develop in his/her children the trust and love that leads to obedience to the parents and to God.

CHAPTER 2

In His Image

*Gen. 1:27 So God created man in his own
image, in the image of God He created him;
male and female He created them.*

If you were asked to organize a talk describing your father, you
would probably spend little time, if any, on his physical description.
Instead, you would likely describe one character attribute after
another, giving examples from his life to illustrate how he was patient
or reckless or kind or whatever personality traits you thought were
characteristic of him. In addition to describing what kind of man he
was, you might talk about him in his career or job and other roles he
played. You would certainly tell what kind of father he was.

I had an opportunity to witness and take part in such an exercise.
When my father died, the three of us children were grown and married
and lived far away. We came together with the rabbi who was to
conduct the service. He did not know my father at all and asked each of
us children and our spouses and my father's widow to tell him about my
father. As we went around the room, each person described character
traits and antidotes that he cherished. Each person had a partial picture
of my father. With all of the comments together, the rabbi knew the
best of my father. In addition, the rabbi got a glimpse into each of us,
for each of us reflected that part of my father we had described.

I talked about his love of learning, remembering how he took me to museums and the Art Institute as I was growing up. I, in turn, took my children to museums and read to them and encouraged their learning. My brother talked about my father's not letting life beat him down, his fighting spirit when things got tough and all odds seemed against him. Years later, my brother fought ALS, Lou Gerhig's Disease, from his chair. He was unable to move in any way, but he would not give up or give in. My brother and sister-in-law's children all have that same spirit in their lives and careers. Knowingly or not, we reflect our parents. Our children are reflections of us.

The kind of person we are and our role as parent are interwoven. We were people before we were parents and we parent as a result of the people we are. Likewise, God is who He is and He parents us as He does because of who He is. He is the parent we should reflect, the parent we want our children to reflect.

There are several benefits of getting to know God and how He is a Father to us. In getting to know God as our father, we learn to appreciate Him, who He is and what He has done for us. We learn to trust Him and to call upon Him. The more we know about God as our Father, the more we can let Him be our example in our parenting. Where we fall short, we can call upon Him to guide us and to make up the difference. We will learn to see ourselves as His children, enabling us to better understand our own children.

It follows that the first chapters of this book deal with who God is and how we are and are not like Him. On first blush, one might be aghast at even comparing ourselves to God, citing Scriptures saying our ways or even our thoughts are not like God's. (Isa. 55:8 "For my thoughts are not your thoughts, neither are your ways my ways," declares the Lord.) Yet the verse that heads this chapter clearly tells us that we are made in His image. Being made in His image, we should reflect His image. What an awesome responsibility. What an awesome privilege.

Chapter 2 examines what it means to be made in God's image and how can we, mere selfish, self absorbed, prideful people ever be able to reflect the image of God. There are really two questions here: What does it mean to be made in God's image? and How we can reflect that image?

We examine first what it means to be made in His image. In chapter 3, we look at how we are not like God and can never be. We must start with both how we are and are not like God because we cannot truly be good parents relying on our own strength and wisdom. It is too difficult and too confusing. Our children have more strength and endurance than we do and society keeps changing the rules. When we recognize the powers of God and how He is and knows and does things we never can, like Job, we will be humbled and reach out to God for His help. He is the perfect parent and we are His imperfect children. It would be hopeless for us imperfect parents to be good parents to our children who are also imperfect were our perfect Father not always with us, waiting for us to call upon Him for help.

Chapter 4 explores God's holiness, His character we can reflect. The different manifestations of holiness that Paul lists are impossible without help of the Holy Spirit. "But the fruit of the Spirit is love, joy, peace, patience, kindness, goodness, faithfulness, gentleness and self-control." (Gal. 5:22-23)

The next few chapters will be looking at these and other attributes. For example, in Chapter 4, we see how we are not like God. This should humble us. Chapter 5 should encourage us to see how the Holy Spirit can, indeed, enable us to reflect God's image, not only in our parenting, but also in everything we do.

Chapter 6 is on the roles God plays. We are to reflect not only who He is, but also what He does, especially in our parenting. While the last half of this book is about God's role as our Father, the role of parent is made up of many other roles.

Part of the difficulty of being a parent is that being a parent means having so many roles in our children's lives. Professionally, people are trained for a job that involves primarily one role. One might be a guidance counselor, or an engineer or a plumber. The preparation is different for a guidance counselor than for someone training to be an engineer. As parents, we have to switch between roles. Sometimes we must take on many roles at once. Yet, the roles we all take at one time or another are the same for all parents.

Ask any parent to write out a job description and, depending on the family structure, you will see chauffeur, cook, laundry man (or laundress), house cleaner, accountant, systems planner, secretary, logistics expert, doctor/nurse, comforter, encourager, coach and several other jobs. Sometimes we are to be shields and protectors, other times we are to be disciplinarians or teachers, still other times playmates or friends.

Although Scripture shows us many attributes of God and tells us we should exhibit them, putting them into practice is, again, something, as imperfect parents, we cannot do in our own strength. We need training as surely as a surgeon does. With all of these jobs, where do we go for training? There are courses to take and books to read. Yet, there are so many books and courses about parenting that it becomes overwhelming. Go to a section in a Christian bookstore on Parenting and there will be more books than most people can read in a year. Some are very good books, with good advice. But the best book on parenting will not be found in that section. It will be over with the bibles.

The bible describes God as our Father. We are told 157 times, mostly in the New Testament, that God is our Father. Everything Jesus said pointed us to our Father. We don't have to go around, as did the rabbi who was doing the service for my father, asking people who God is and what kind of a Father He is. He has told us Himself. It's in our bibles. The bible is our guidebook. So we learn about God in our bibles and look there to Him for advice and for our role model in our parenting. Understanding the roles God plays in our lives enables us to fill these roles in our children's.

Being made in His image means that, with the Holy Spirit's help, we can reflect Him in all we do, especially in our parenting.

CHAPTER 3

We are Not God

Isa. 55:8 For my thoughts are not your thoughts,
neither are your ways my ways, declares the Lord.

It is almost laughable to think we are like God, eternal, omniscient, omnipresent, omnipotent, unless you ask a small child. Small children think their parents are eternal, or at least that they have been around since before computers. Being unable to imagine life without their parents, small children think their parents will be around forever too. Many children think their mothers are all-knowing. A mother can be busy cleaning a bathroom when the child decides it is the perfect opportunity to sneak a cookie or two. Just as the lid is ever so gently lifted from the jar, the mother's voice rings out, "What are you doing? You had better not be getting a cookie. It's too close to dinner." A friend's teenage son told her that when encouraged to do something he knew was wrong, he'd answer that he wouldn't because his mom *always* finds out. To our children, especially to the young ones, we are omniscient.

Likewise, fathers are omniscient and omnipotent to children. A father can ride a bike and know the right tool to fix something that is broken. If there is a bully in the neighborhood or school, Dad can take care of it. Fathers have the power to face anything.

This awesome adoration might last until adolescence. At that point, parents lose their godlike status and their place as a source of authority. If rebellion hasn't started before this point, it often starts at adolescence. Most teenagers can and will be happy to tell an inquiring parent how he or she falls short.

This chapter deals with falling short. Even the best-intentioned parents fall short. We advise children with imperfect knowledge or out of our own prejudices, often steering them wrong. We cannot see the future or advise them with any certainty regarding it, although we try. With the technological advances and the change in the moral compass of this country, in many ways this world is very unlike that in which most of us spent childhood and our youth. For some of us there were no computers. There are now so many different ways our children can sit in a chair, transfixed, today. That is not only bad for their bodies, but it is frightening to think what their minds are being fed while they stare at the screen. Through their computers, they have more information at their fingertips than we had in whole libraries. Parents who don't know the potential for good and for evil on the web cannot advise their children on its use in any meaningful way.

If you have not visited your child's school to observe classmates and talk to teachers and administrators, you cannot know the pressures under which your child lives 6 to 8 hours a day, five days a week. Your advice based on your childhood experiences is hopelessly obsolete. People haven't changed. There are still godly and ungodly people. But the world has changed and is changing too fast for us to guide our children through each decision and every attack of the enemy.

Likewise, parents often advise their children from their own prejudices, insisting a child go in one academic direction or another, rather than allowing the child to discover his/her own talents. Our prejudices against groups of people, because of their cultural, racial or religious background can keep our children from forming meaningful relationships and being God's light in this dark world.

We give them rules for our own convenience instead of for their good. We get tired and cranky and short tempered. The most difficult shortcoming we have as earthly parents is that we know we cannot save them from themselves or protect them when they are not with us. The older they grow, the less time they spend with their parents. When they are at school, with friends, wherever, we cannot be there to whisper in their ear about a bad or dangerous decision they are about to make. No matter how perfect a parent we try to be, our humanity will get in the way, and we will fall short.

We must understand what God is like in ways we are not so that we will know to call upon Him when our own resources run dry. This chapter discusses five attributes of God. The first two are necessary for the other three because the first two attributes, eternality and immutability, are part of the other three, omniscience, omnipresence, and omnipotence. Because God is without beginning or end and He was, He is, and He will always be the same (Heb. 13:8), God is also all knowing, ever present, and all-powerful. The qualities of eternality, omniscience and omnipresence are ones that enable God, in His wisdom, to help us in our parenting.

God is eternal. We measure time by the movement of the earth around the sun. We have a solar calendar. Other cultures measure time by the movement of the moon around the earth. They use lunar calendars. The book of John begins with, "In the beginning was the Word, and the Word was with God, and the Word was God." (Jn. 1:1) It is a beginning before there was time. We know that God existed before time because He created the means by which we measure time, the sun, moon, stars and planets. As the Creator, He exists today and will exist forever, irrespective of whether the earth and sun and moon exist.

We know from Scripture that God is eternal. He had no beginning as we understand beginnings and He has no end. The psalmist says, "From everlasting to everlasting Thou art God" (Ps. 90:2). He is called the Eternal God in both Genesis (Gen. 21:33) and Deuteronomy (Deut. 33:37). Isaiah tells us, "Trust in the Lord forever, for the Lord, the Lord, is the Rock eternal." (Is. 26:4). And Paul writes to Timothy, "Now to the King eternal, immortal, invisible, the only God, be honor and glory for ever and ever."(1Tim. 1:17).

Although our physical bodies will have an end, human beings have eternity before us, an eternity we can only imagine from the descriptions in the Bible. All those who believe Jesus was the Son of God who died to pay the price for our sin, as promised in the Old Testament, will live eternally with Him. (John 3:16) We do not, however, have an eternity behind us. Although God knew us before we were conceived, (Ps. 2:10,71:16, 139:13; Isa. 49:1, Jer. 1:5), we each did have a beginning. We were conceived and we were born. Most of us have no memory of events before we were two years old, much less before we were born. We are not eternal in the same sense God is.

What does it mean to us that God is eternal? It is not His eternality itself, but Who He is because of His eternality that is important to us. Because He is eternal, He can be both omniscient, that is, all knowing, and omnipresent, that is always present. If God were bound in any way by time, He could not be all knowing. The part of time that was beyond his existence would be as unknowable for Him as the future is for us. God could not be present in the spectrum of time in which He did not exist. He is not the god of an age, but was with Adam and is with us, and will be present when the earth as we know it ends.

God is also immutable, that is unchanging. As He says, "I the Lord do not change."(Mal. 3:6). Through James, His Spirit tells us, "Every good and perfect gift is from above, coming down from the Father of the heavenly lights, who does not change like shifting shadows." (James 1:17). This is important because we need a rock on which we build our faith. (Matt. 7:24-26)

There is no certainty and no security in a god who changes the rules or changes his promises. As people we change, and we must be thankful for that; but God does not change. We can trust His word and use it as our guidebook because what it demands, what it promises and that it never changes.

Thank Him that He made us able to change. We change throughout our lives. We change in every way, physically, mentally, emotionally and spiritually. Our physical changes are obvious, although they are not obvious to many people. We like to think what is will always be. A ten year old does not look at himself and see the future grown man or woman, much less the future old man or woman. We adults have trouble when we realize our bodies never stop changing. As parents, we need to help our children understand their own bodies, the stage they are in and the physical changes they will soon encounter. And we need to be realistic about our own physical changes as we age.

Our mental and emotional changes are also obvious. No one is born knowing right from wrong or knowing how to read. And, when a preteen declares he or she is in love, we parents know there is a long way to go in the child's emotional maturation before we are willing to accept such a declaration. It takes emotional maturity for a youngster to see that it is in his best interest to share or wait his turn. Some people become adults without ever reaching that level of maturity. Yet, thankfully, most of us mature and change physically and emotionally as we age.

We must grow and change spiritually as well. We came into the world with a sin nature. (Ps. 51:5) "Surely I was sinful at birth, sinful from the time my mother conceived me." And we know that apart from God, we cannot change in our spiritual maturity. (Rom. 7:18) "I know that nothing good lives in me, that is, in my sinful nature. For I have the desire to do what is good, but I cannot carry it out." As we mature in our faith, we are to become ever more like our Savior. (Rom. 8:29, Phil. 3:10, 1Jn. 4:17) God desires that the change within us is complete. Paul wrote the Ephesians that we are to put off the old person we were and rise to a new life "created to be like God in true righteousness and holiness." (Eph. 4:22-24)

God does not need to change because God is already perfect. He is perfect in an absolute sense and He is perfect in the sense of being complete unto Himself. Jesus commanded us, "Be perfect, therefore, as your heavenly Father is perfect."(Matt. 5:48). We can trust Him and His word, the bible, because God does not change, like shifting sand.

Becoming more like God, becoming complete in Him, is a process. Most of us take two steps forward and one step back as we mature. Practically speaking for our parenting, it means we will fail as we, little by little, put off the old self. As we do, we must admit to our children our shortcomings, asking forgiveness instead of justifying our mistakes. They must see we are growing just as they are growing and that we all have the same standard, God's, which does not change.

As I said before, without God's eternality and immutability, He could not be all knowing or ever present throughout all time. If He was bound by time or was changeable, He could know some things, but not all things, could be with us for a time but not with every generation throughout time. If God were not eternal and immutable, He could be all-powerful for a time, but could not be omnipotent all the time.

God is omniscient. Knowledge begins with Him. (Job 21:22) "Can anyone teach knowledge to God, since he judges even the highest?" All we know, God has enabled and allowed us to discover. "For the Lord gives wisdom, and from his mouth come knowledge and understanding." (Prov. 2:6) Because He is eternal, He can see events long past, ones of which we are not even aware. He can see the future results of choices we may not even have made yet. Even when our children are with us, we cannot always know what they need for their long-term well being. Only God knows the future and the impact of the past and present on it.

God is omnipresent. He promised us through Moses and Joshua that He would never leave us or forsake us. (Deut. 31:6, Deut. 31:8, Josh. 1:5). He is ever present. (Ps. 46:1) "God is our refuge and strength, an ever-present help in trouble." In Hebrews we are promised that His angels will watch over us. "Are not all angels ministering spirits sent to serve those who will inherit salvation?" (Heb. 1:14)

Furthermore, God is with us directly as the Holy Spirit. John the Baptist told the people and us, "I baptize you with water, but He will baptize you with the Holy Spirit." (Mark 1:8) Jesus told us that God in the person of the Holy Spirit would be with us forever. (Jn. 14:16) "And I will ask the Father, and He will give you another Counselor to be with you forever." We know that promise was not just for the apostles and disciples who were with Jesus, because through Peter, God assured us, "Repent and be baptized, every one of you, in the name of Jesus Christ for the forgiveness of your sins. And you will receive the gift of the Holy Spirit." (Acts 2:38)

God is Omnipotent. He is all-powerful. He created the stars and the planets, the earth and all that is on and in and around it, (Gen 1, 2) He opened the Sea of Reeds (Ex.) and the Jordan River (Josh. 4:23-24). God even stopped the earth in its course so the sun seemed to stand still (Josh. 10:12-13). God entered the womb of a virgin. God made natural law and can abridge it. There is nothing beyond the power of God.

God is all knowing, but we are not. Yet, we can call upon Him, in His wisdom and knowledge to help guide us. In fact, we are told to do so. "If any of you lacks wisdom, he should ask God, who gives generously to all without finding fault, and it will be given to him." (James 1:5) Many times I have cried out to God for wisdom, not knowing what to do for or about one of our children or our grandchildren. I don't know what to say to our children or grandchildren who are grown and don't know God. I don't know how hard to push when I know they seem to be headed in a direction we think is wrong. God, in His infinite knowledge and wisdom, sometimes says to leave the children in His hands. He sometimes through the Holy Spirit convicts me of my need to control everything, especially my children. He gives me the words, always just the right words when I call upon Him for help. I don't have the wisdom that comes with being all knowing, but He does, and He wants us to ask Him for help.

What a comfort to know that God is all knowing and ever present. We cannot be with our children all the time. When they are little, we hire sitters or ask family to watch them. When they are older, they go to school. Even home-schooled children go off and play with friends. The older the children are, the longer and farther away they go. Yet, God is always with our children to fill the needs that He knows are within His plan for them. He is also always with us to listen to our prayers for our children. That is what it means to us that He is all knowing and ever present and all-powerful. We can't be in two or more places at once, but God can and is. He knows our needs and our children's needs and He can provide for those needs that are in His plan.

There is nothing beyond Him. I have seen God change heart attitudes and mend broken hearts. I have seen and have met people whom God miraculously saved from the jaws of certain death. God can protect our children when we can't. He can protect our children when we don't even know they need protection. God can do this because He is all knowing, ever present and all-powerful.

An example of this in my own life happened after two miscarriages. I had a difficult pregnancy with our last child. I prayed unceasingly for our unborn son. I was full term and the baby was in the right position, but had not dropped. The doctor had me go to the hospital for the fetal heartbeat to be monitored about one hour every other day and then see him the intervening days. He was usually was not in the hospital during the tests, since no one expected anything dramatic. The second or third such test day, he happened to be in the hospital delivering another baby when my baby's heartbeat dropped from about 124 beats a minute to 28 beats a minute. The nurse grabbed the doctor as he headed into the delivery room. He ordered oxygen and, when he heard the drop in heart rate was coincident with the tinniest of twinges of a contraction, he ordered me prepped for an emergency cesarean section. God was protecting our baby. The doctor said, after delivering him, that the chord had been wrapped so tightly around his throat a single strong contraction would have strangled him. I was 2 weeks over due.

One verse declaring God's promise encourages me when my role as parent seems overwhelming. At times I want so badly to guide or do for my children, but I can't. Those times I turn to God and claim His promise, "And we know that God causes all things to work together for good to those who love God, to those who are called according to His purpose. (Rom. 8:28,) This does not mean that God will keep all bad things out of our children's lives. It means that there is nothing in their lives that He can or will not work for the good, for those who love Him. That, of course is the key. We must show our children that we love God and teach them to love Him too.

As Christians, we all need to live with the promise of Romans 8:28 and to help our children learn it and live by it. We and they must know that God can and will cause even the worst circumstances to work together for the good for those who love Him. We parents cannot make that promise. Only God can.

We are not eternal or immutable. We are not omniscient, omnipresent or omnipotent. Knowing we can never be God should be a relief. We can't do it well and right on our own. We do not have to do it on our own. Indeed, God doesn't want us to try to do it on our own. He wants us to turn to Him for help in our parenting, just as He wants us to turn to Him in everything we do. (Is. 45:22, Matt. 6:35, 1Pet. 4:11)

CHAPTER 4

His Character We Strive For

*Rom. 8:29 For those God foreknew he also
predestined to be conformed to the likeness of his Son*

We are to be conformed to the likeness of Jesus, God incarnate. This chapter examines what that means for us, mere humans. We will look at God's character traits that, with the help of the Holy Spirit, will transform us bit by bit to be more like Him, especially in raising our children.

We begin with God's promise to help us develop His qualities and the one condition under which He says He will help. Jesus said, "If you love me, you will obey what I command. And I will ask the Father, and He will give you another Counselor (helper) to be with you forever —the Spirit of Truth. The world cannot accept him, because it neither sees him nor knows him. But you know him, for He lives with you and will be in you." (Jn. 14:15-17)

This is a conditional promise. Jesus prefaces the promise of the Holy Spirit, who will be with us and in us with the condition that first we must love Him. Jesus tells us that our obedience will spring from our love, as surely as our children's obedience will grow as they learn to love and trust us.

If we love God, we will bear fruit of the Spirit who is within us. "But the fruit of the Spirit is love, joy, peace, patience, kindness, goodness, faithfulness, gentleness and self-control." (Gal. 5:22-23) These attributes will define us to the rest of the world as Christians, and will, of course, be important in our roles as parents. When we have peace and patience and self-control when others are wringing their hands and are all upset, we stand out. When we love those who have hurt us and return their hurt with gentleness, kindness and goodness, we stand out.

These qualities are called fruit of the Spirit because only with the help of the Spirit can we consistently bear His fruit. These characteristics are not typical of the world. The world teaches us to love and value ourselves first. We live with expressions like, "What's in it for me?' Road rage, for instance, is the epitome of selfishness and lack of self-control.

Yet, even people who are far from God do nice things. One does not need to love God to be nice to people who are nice to them. Jesus told us, (Matt. 5:44-47) "But I tell you: Love your enemies and pray for those who persecute you, that you may be sons of your Father in heaven. He causes his sun to rise on the evil and the good, and sends rain on the righteous and the unrighteous. If you love those who love you, what reward will you get? Are not even the tax collectors doing that? And if you greet only your brothers, what are you doing more than others? Do not even pagans do that?"

Jesus says here that when we love those who are our enemies and those who make our lives unhappy, we are showing the world we are children of our Father. It is not enough to be nice to those who are nice to us or have our sympathies.

When Jesus says we are to love our enemies, there are those who might ask, "How do I do that?" Luke reports Jesus' words. He gave us a clear picture of a love we can only achieve with the help of the Spirit. (Lk. 6:27-31) "But I tell you who hear me: Love your enemies, do good to those who hate you, bless those who curse you, pray for those who mistreat you. If someone strikes you on one cheek, turn to him the other also. If someone takes your cloak, do not stop him from taking your tunic. Give to everyone who asks you, and if anyone takes what belongs to you, do not demand it back. Do to others as you would have them do to you."

These are radical ideas and commandments. We are not only to pray for our enemies, we are to do good to those who hate us. A tsunami that devastated Southeast Asia provided the Christians of the world the opportunity to show the world exactly what Jesus commanded us. The people of Southeast Asia are predominantly Moslem, Hindu and Buddhist. They have been perpetrators of Christian persecution. The human thing to do was to turn our backs on them, our enemies. Yet, that is not what organizations like Samaritan's Purse and Salvation Army and Habitat for Humanity and so many other Christian organizations did.

Love, joy, peace, patience, kindness, goodness, faithfulness, gentleness and self-control are attributes that will make us stand out in the world. They are also important in our roles as parents. But God has a great many other attributes we need to try to reflect to be the parents He wants us to be. Many of them I also incorporate into the chapters on His role of Father. For example, God is compassionate. (Ps. 145:9) "The Lord is good to all; he has compassion on all he has made." When we account for our children's limitations, we reflect God's compassion on us. When we set standards and hold our children to those standards, we must be just and fair, even as our Father is with us. (2Ths. 1:6) "God is just." and (Prov. 3:12) "because the Lord disciplines those He loves, as a father the son he delights in." And we must be forgiving, for we know we fall short too. (Eph. 4:32) "Be kind and compassionate to one another, forgiving each other, just as in Christ God forgave you."

There is one attribute of God that encompasses all of this. This attribute will affect and define our lives in the world around us, and especially with our spouses and children. Above all, God is holy. (Ps. 77:13) "Your ways, O God, are holy. What god is so great as our God?" and (Ps. 99:3) "Let them praise your great and awesome name — He is holy." and (Isa. 6:3) "Holy, holy, holy is the Lord Almighty; the whole earth is full of his glory."

Webster defines the holiness as spiritually pure and set apart. Jesus was spiritually pure. He was without sin. (Heb. 4:15)

Obviously, we cannot on our own be spiritually pure or perfect as our Father is perfect. None of in our own flesh can honestly say we are without sin. (Ps. 143:2) "No one living is righteous before you." and (Rom. 3:23) "for all have sinned and fall short of the glory of God" and, again, (1Jn 1:8) "If we claim to be without sin, we deceive ourselves and the truth is not in us."

Still, we are called repeatedly to be holy. (Lev. 20:26) "You are to be holy to me because I, the Lord, am holy, and I have set you apart from the nations to be my own." and (Lev. 21:8) "I the Lord am holy —I who make you holy." and (1Pet. 1:15-16) "But just as He who called you is holy, so be holy in all you do" for it is written: "Be holy, because I am holy."

Our being holy is not as impossible as it sounds, although we can never be as holy as God. In 1Peter, God repeats the charge for us to be holy. Only God can make us holy. That is why Jesus had to come and die to pay the price for our sin and cleanse us, as He promised. (1Jn 1:9) "If we confess our sins, He is faithful and just and will forgive us our sins and purify us from all unrighteousness." He came to set us apart and make us spiritually pure.

What does it mean for us to be holy and what does it have to do with our parenting? When God calls us to be holy, to be set apart and spiritually pure, He is talking about our hearts being pure, and He is also talking about our behavior. Just as Paul wrote of the fruits of the Spirit, he also wrote of what living an unholy life looks like. (Gal. 5:19-21) "The acts of the sinful nature are obvious: sexual immorality, impurity and debauchery; idolatry and witchcraft; hatred, discord, jealousy, fits of rage, selfish ambition, dissensions, factions and envy; drunkenness, orgies, and the like."

These behaviors come from spiritually impure hearts, hearts bound by sin. I cannot imagine any of you readers practicing witchcraft or participating in orgies, but the others signs of the world are sins all too common even among Christians. Hatred, jealousy, selfish ambition, and envy spring from the sins of an impure heart. Our behavior is the result of our heart attitudes. (Matt. 15:18) "But the things that come out of the mouth come from the heart, and these make a man 'unclean."

There is no sin that does not affect other people. Once I had been terribly wronged and was very angry for a long time. My anger affected everyone around me, especially my children. The wrong I had suffered consumed my thoughts. There was no room for God's love and peace. When I finally asked Christ to help me forgive with the forgiveness He paid for, if not my own even, I was able to let it go. Forgiveness brings freedom. What an overwhelming sense of God's love filled me then. There was room for joy again. And it brought freedom to my children. No longer did they worry about taking sides or about talking to me about their father. When I had condemned their father, I was condemning part of them. We are all so thankful that ended.

When people are consumed with hatred or jealousy or selfish ambition, it will be reflected in their behavior, just as mine was. Certainly it will lead to discord. Perhaps it will also lead to drunkenness, or lying or slandering, or some other sin. Our sins show through our behavior and often our children are the first to sense them and suffer from them.

All of us from time to time may find ourselves envious or acting out of selfishness, or causing dissension. We are human and we sin. Yet, if our behavior reflects these consistently, we show the world, and especially our children, that we do not walk with God. (1Jn. 3:6) "No one who lives in Him keeps on sinning. No one who continues to sin has either seen Him or known Him."

We may find all sorts of ways to justify our sins, but sin will always be sin. God and His rules are the same yesterday, today and tomorrow. We may try to kid ourselves and justify ourselves, but if we are honest, we will know that it is no fun to sin. It is like being in prison in solitary confinement, separated from God. Our sins will separate us from our children even as we are separated from our Father. However, we can set those sins aside with the help of the Holy Spirit. (Jn. 8:34) "I tell you the truth, everyone who sins is a slave to sin. Now a slave has no permanent place in the family, but a son belongs to it forever. So if the Son sets you free, you will be free indeed." God will free us to be His children and live blameless lives.

Above all, we are living examples to our children of how to behave, just as Jesus is our living example. Children learn much more from watching than from listening. The old saying, "Do as I say, not as I do," goes nowhere with children. They all seem to have hypocrisy detectors. So in our daily lives, we are to lean upon the Holy Spirit to help us change. (1Cor. 10:13) "No temptation has seized you except what is common to man. And God is faithful; He will not let you be tempted beyond what you can bear. But when you are tempted, He will also provide a way out so that you can stand up under it."

But being a living example of holiness is not just a list of what we must not do, envy, worry, profane God's name, steal, etc. It is a positive life style. We began this chapter with the list of the fruits of the Spirit: Love, joy, peace, patience, kindness, goodness, faithfulness, gentleness and self-control. Behaviors that spring from the Fruits will set us apart. We will be living holiness. And this list of fruits, of heart attitudes, all spring from embracing merely two commandments. (Mark 12:30-31) "Love the Lord your God with all your heart and with all your soul and with all your mind and with all your strength.' The second is this: 'Love your neighbor as yourself.' There is no commandment greater than these."

So we begin and end this chapter with the need for us to love. Love is an active verb. They see holiness in us not just when our children know we say "No" to R-rated movies, but when they see us give credit to and praise God for our abilities and opportunities, when they hear us pray aloud for people they know have hurt us, when they feel our love and forgiveness when they stumble and fall. There are so many opportunities to reflect God's holiness. This is something we can do, with the help of Him who made us.

I have a friend who told her children as they were growing up, "We are not like other people. We are Christians and will live as Christians. So don't bother coming home and telling me that so and so is doing something and you want to do it too. I don't care what any one else is doing. My answer will be "Is it right? Is it good?" The Bible calls us to be different, and we will be."

It is an awesome responsibility and privilege to be a parent. It is the most difficult job we will ever have, and there is no retiring from it. Furthermore, none of us have either perfect earthly role models or inner resources to do the job well by ourselves. We must be thankful we have a perfect role model in God, our Father, a handbook He has written to help us, and the Holy Spirit to guide and enable us to, little by little, be conformed to the image of His Son. We must be thankful He has promised to be there to help us whenever we call, whenever we are ready to listen. We don't have to and we can't be the parents God wants us to be alone.

CHAPTER 5

The Hats Our Father Wears

*Deut. 32:26 Is he not your Father, your
Creator, who made you and formed you?*

This book focuses on God, our Father. We all know that being a parent involves many roles. If we look at the roles we have with our children as parents, we see that God has many of those same roles with us. In this chapter we look at two of the roles, creator and teacher, and at how God fulfills them. These roles are reflected in all other roles God has in our lives and that we have in our children's lives. In this chapter we look at how we can learn from Him to fulfill those roles for our children.

The first and most obvious role is that God is our creator. For many people it is not difficult to believe that God created the heaven and earth, just as is recounted in Genesis 1 and 2. In part, because we know the facts of the birds and the bees, the nitty-gritty of the biology of how babies are conceived, many people have a hard time placing God in our own creation. Yet, King David declares that God formed him as he was growing within his mother and that He was instrumental in David's birth. (Ps. 139:13) "For You created my inmost being; You knit me together in my mother's womb." (Ps. 22:9-10) "Yet You brought me out of the womb; You made me trust in You even at my mother's breast. From birth I was cast upon

You; from my mother's womb You have been my God." And Moses rebukes the Israelites who have been complaining throughout their forty years of wandering in the desert even as God provided for them. (Deut. 32: 26) "Is this the way you repay the Lord, O foolish and unwise people? Is he not your Father, your Creator, who made you and formed you?"

We all know how it feels to make something with great care and love. It may be something that is not important to any one else in the world, but to us it is. It is our creation. Perhaps it is something sewn or baked. Perhaps it is something out of wood or a picture or a poem or letter written, or a musical piece played or even a special pile of rocks arranged just so. When we create something, it becomes a part of us and we put ourselves into it. It is our creation. And when we know we have done a good job, we get much pleasure.

It is just so for God. On the sixth day God created man and woman. (Gen. 1:27) He breathed into them the Spirit of Life. (Gen. 2:7) He looked at what He created and He saw that it was good. (Gen. 1:31) As David wrote, He gave each of us the breath of life. He created us. And if we, mere humans, can have affection and pleasure from inanimate things we make, how much greater pleasure we should have in the creation of life. How much more intimate can one feel than the oneness of the creator and what has been created?

We are our children's human creators. They are not merely by products of our love for our spouses or our pleasure. Male and female each takes part of himself to create an entirely new human being. And because environment has such great influence on how a person grows, our part in their creation only begins with conception.

God makes us aware that, as God's unique creation, each of us has a special place in His heart. Likewise, we must not only treasure our children in the same way, we must let them know we treasure them. In Psalm 136 alone, through David, God tells us in every line, 26 times, that His love for us endures forever.

It is easy to see our children's shortcomings. In our house, we needed only look at the condition of our younger son's room or look at what he'd left outdoors on the lawn or in the family room to be aware he walked off and left things without caring. How many times had he been told that was not being a good steward of what had been given him? As God does with us, while not letting the faults slide, we reassured him of our love, yet let him know when he was doing wrong.

We are all created in the image of God. (Gen. 1:27, Gen. 9:6) Not only in the image of God, our children are created in our image. We must let them know they are treasured.

Another obvious role God takes for us that we take for our children is teacher. When a child is born, he knows nothing. A baby must learn even who his parents are, just as we must learn to know our Father. God said, "Therefore I will teach them — this time I will teach them my power and might. Then they will know that My name is the Lord." (Jer. 16:21)

We human beings are such slow learners. Let's look at how God taught the Israelites, and taught them over and over again. God taught them His care and His power when He brought them out of slavery. (Ex. 1-15) When God sustained them in the desert for forty years, He taught them He was their provider and that their lives depended on trusting Him.

From the time they entered the Promised Land until the Babylonian captivity, they repeatedly forgot God's lesson that their lives depended on trusting Him. Time and again they turned to other, man-made, gods and turned away from God's laws about how to treat one another. God removed His hedge of protection until they cried out to Him in desperation. He rescued them time and again and protected them until they again turned away from Him. (Josh.-Mal.) By the time of Jeremiah, God had divided the nation of Israel into the nations of Judah and Israel. First Israel turned to Baal. Then Judah turned. In the desert, God taught the descendants of Israel (Jacob) He would provide for them. Throughout the Old Testament, He also taught them He would enforce the consequences of their turning to other gods for protection. Discipline is the part of parenting addressed in Chapter 12, Keeping Your Word.

Like God teaching us, we must teach our children what it means to them that we are their parents. It is not that we have power over them, but that we have the power to love them, to keep them safe under normal circumstances, the power to provide for their physical, emotional and spiritual well being, as well as the power to enforce the rules we make for their own good.

There are physical things we teach, of course. As a child grows, every age has it's things to master. A baby must learn to eat with utensils. A toddler learns to walk and run. As they grow older the things they must learn are more complex. They learn to tie shoes and to read and write and use a computer. We teach them how to take care of themselves, how to dress themselves, how to cook and keep themselves clean, how to drive and, we all hope, how to make good decisions and stay out of trouble.

God also teaches us how to live. Isaiah tell us, "This is what the Lord says — your Redeemer, the Holy One of Israel: I am the Lord your God, who teaches you what is best for you, who directs you in the way you should go." (Isa. 48:17) Throughout the Bible, God tells us specifics of how to live. David writes, "Good and upright is the Lord; therefore he instructs sinners in his ways. He guides the humble in what is right and teaches them his way."(Ps. 25:8-9) We are told many times throughout the Bible that God is our teacher, if we will only humble ourselves to listen.

The Book of Proverbs is God's instruction through Solomon to all of us for our day to day living. "The proverbs of Solomon son of David, king of Israel: for attaining wisdom and discipline; for understanding words of insight; for acquiring a disciplined and prudent life, doing what is right and just and fair; for giving prudence to the simple, knowledge and discretion to the young —let the wise listen and add to their learning, and let the discerning get guidance —for understanding proverbs and parables, the sayings and riddles of the wise." (Prov.1: 1-6)

These instructions are for our everyday behavior. For example, 15 verses in Proverbs tell us to guard our tongues. How many times have we told our children to say, "Please" and "Thank you", or to be quiet or that what they had just said was not nice? How many times have we found ourselves speaking out in anger or gossip, and later regretting it? In Proverbs, as throughout the Bible, we are warned about choosing friends wisely, about infidelity, drunkenness, and so many other things that may touch our lives on a daily basis.

While we tend to rebel from time to time against God's instructions of how to live, we ultimately know that what He teaches us is for our own good. As Paul wrote, "I am saying this for your own good, not to restrict you, but that you may live in a right way in undivided devotion to the Lord." (1Cor. 7:35)

Likewise, our instruction and rules for our children must be for their own good. We teach them to pick up after themselves, for example, primarily because we know that is how they can take care of and preserve their things, being good stewards of what they have been given. Having our children put away their own things also helps them keep track of their things so that they later can find them. Putting things away also teaches them the responsibility to be accountable for all of their actions. A by-product is a neater, more comfortable house for the parents, but the underlying purpose of those rules is to teach our children to take care of themselves in ways that honor God and are for their own long-term benefit. As parents, it is important for us to take the time to explain to our children why our rules are for their good.

People tend to have two different reactions to God's instructions of how we should live, just as different children have different reactions to their parent's rules. We can obey or we can rebel. There are both children and adults who reject parental authority and rebel against rules. We know what God thinks of that. As Jesus said, "You are the ones who justify yourselves in the eyes of men, but God knows your hearts. What is highly valued among men is detestable in God's sight." (Lk. 16:15) I don't know a single parent who has an easy time accepting the actions of a rebellious child.

Invariably, those who are rebellious have found ways to justify their rebellion. God says it's as if they are blind. They inevitably get into trouble at some point. For those who rebel against our Father's authority, the boom will fall when they finally have to face Him. In the here and now, in human terms, these people may look successful. We may not see the consequences of their rebellion, but God warns us all, "You say, 'I am rich; I have acquired wealth and do not need a thing.' But you do not realize that you are wretched, pitiful, poor, blind and naked." (Rev. 3:17)

Likewise, our children can often get away with breaking rules in the short term, sneaking the extra cookie, cheating on a test, staying out after curfew, shoplifting. We have to impress upon them that they are harming themselves. Even if they don't get caught, someday they will be held responsible for the material on the test. Even if they do not get caught, they will always have to be afraid they will be discovered. They will be tired after staying out. They will live with the knowledge they have no right to own what they have shoplifted and be afraid of being apprehended. We must let them know, that even if they seem to get away with it in man's eyes, they will know they have done wrong and God will know and hold them accountable.

Others are rebellious because they are ignorant of the rules. "Why didn't you say so?" "I didn't know you wanted me to do that." "I didn't know it was against the rules." Again, God is our role model. We have no excuse of not knowing what God wants of us. As Jesus said of the Pharisees, "If I had not come and spoken to them, they would not be guilty of sin. Now, however, they have no excuse for their sin." (Jn. 15:22) Chapter 10 is about articulating the rules and their consequences so our children have no excuse of ignorance.

The most important instruction we can give our children is about the trinity, God, our Father, Jesus, our Savior, and the Holy Spirit. We are to tell them from our own experience so that they will know. "Only be careful, and watch yourselves closely so that you do not forget the things your eyes have seen or let them slip from your heart as long as you live. Teach them to your children and to their children after them." (Deut.4:9) We will be held accountable if we don't teach them about God. (Deut.11:19) "Teach them to your children, talking about them when you sit at home and when you walk along the road, when you lie down and when you get up."

The entire reason for this book is that our children's obedience both to God and to us parents springs from trusting, trusting that all the rules of God are for our good and that our rules for our children are for their own good. They must be obedient to us, whom they can see, first, before they can learn to be obedient to God. We must teach them the reasons for our hope and joy and teach them through words and example, the path to heaven. "Though you have not seen Him, you love Him; and even though you do not see Him now, you believe in Him and are filled with an inexpressible and glorious joy, for you are receiving the goal of your faith, the salvation of your souls." (1Pet. 1:8-9)

There are other roles, of course, that are tied up with being a parent.

Through out the rest of the book, we look more closely at these other roles that we play in our children's lives that our Father plays in ours. We can learn from Him how to best fulfill these roles.

CHAPTER 6

Unconditional Love

*Ps.100:5 For the Lord is good and his
love endures forever; his faithfulness
continues through all generations.*

Unconditional love means that God's love for us is not dependent upon us, on how we feel, believe or behave. He loves us because He made us and has chosen to love us. As Psalm 136 says, His love endures <u>forever</u>. There is nothing we can do to get Him to stop loving us. Unconditional love is the central feature of building trust because upon it rests all the other elements. That is, if we are certain we cannot lose our Father's love no matter how far we stray or how often we stumble, we will trust that what He tells us to do is out of His love for us.

We know His love is unconditional because He says it is, as in Psalm 136. In addition, throughout the bible He shows us that He doesn't desert His children, even when they mistrust, disobey, or turn away from Him. In our own lives, we can also see His unfailing love.

We can see an example of this unfailing love in the way God reacted to Abraham's lack of faith. With faith Abraham left Haran and went where God led him, for which he is held as an example to us in Hebrews 11: 8-10. Yet, when a famine struck Canaan,

Abraham did not trust God to sustain and protect him. He went to Egypt, and he told his wife, Sarai, that if she didn't lie and say that she was his sister and let them take her for Pharaoh's harem, the Egyptians would kill him to get her. God had already promised him in Gen. 12:2 that He would make him a great nation. Abraham did not trust God enough to think God would protect him.

God could have been angry. In essence, He could have thrown up His hands and said, "Abraham, if you don't trust me to keep my promises and if you take matters in you own hands, there's no point in going on. You won't have your heir or the land. I'll pick someone else."

That was exactly my reaction when our younger son took matters into his own hands. I told him, for example, that I would get something for him that I knew was impossible or dangerous for him to reach, or that I would help him do something for which I knew he needed help. Usually I was in the middle of something when I became aware that he needed my help. Often he wouldn't wait for me. He tried to get it or do it and invariably got into trouble. He'd get frustrated or hurt himself or break something. In my flesh I'd yell at him, "Why didn't you wait for me? Do you think that I wasn't going to ever get around to helping when I said I would?" I sometimes would tell him to go ahead and get it for himself, even though I knew that would only bring him more trouble. Or sometimes I even took back my permission for him to get or do what I had offered to help with in the first place.

That is not how God responded to Abraham. At the same time Abraham was not trusting God, God was rescuing Abraham by causing serious illness to inflict Pharaoh and his household. (Gen. 12:17) It is important to see, though, God also allowed Abraham to suffer the consequences of his actions. The wealth with which Pharaoh sent out Abram and Lot caused dissension between them. (Gen. 13:5-12)

Our younger son not waiting for me showed he didn't trust me to help him. His lack of trust made me angry, and in my flesh

I responded with anger. I should have responded to him as God responded to Abraham. I should have let my son know I was disappointed and that what happened was the result of his decision not to wait. If there was a mess, I should have required him clean it up. I should not have yelled at him or made him feel unloved. It was important for him to know I loved him even when he did things that were wrong.

Not waiting seems like such a little thing compared to what children can get into and do these days. Like the Israelites in the Promised Land, they are surrounded by ungodly people and images and words. We are bombarded with messages everywhere we turn that some product is all we need to make us happy, that we must buy it. We are surrounded by movies, books, television and on the computer in which homosexuality, extramarital sex, profanity and violence are assumed to be normal. The culture of the country says there are no absolutes and everyone is to do what is right for himself.

Many youth are doing just that. We know several families in which children are battling with drugs. When our neighbor's son was a sophomore in high school, he was planning to attend the university in our town. When I asked him whether he'd live at home or on campus, he replied, "I'll live at home until I get a girlfriend. Then I'll move in with her." It is not condemned by our culture. We have five adult children. All but one of them lived with a partner before being married. People are doing what is right in their own eyes.

The question is, what are we parents to do about our wayward children? We can learn from the parable of the Prodigal Son how to and not to react when our children go astray (Lk. 15:11-24). This parable is the last of three that Jesus tells regarding how our Father rejoices each time one of us returns to Him. He has just finished telling the parables of the lost sheep and the lost coin,

"Jesus continued: 'There was a man who had two sons. The younger one said to his father, 'Father, give me my share of the estate.' So he divided his property between them. Not long after that, the younger son got together all he had, set off for a distant country and there squandered his wealth in wild living." (Lk. 15:11-13)

Can you imagine how hurt the father was? Yet, the father does not prevent his younger son from leaving. He could have refused to give his son the inheritance and the son would not have been able to go. When our children are determined to stray, we must let them go. As much as it hurts, some children must experience the evil of the world before they can recognize the goodness of living with God.

Nor does the father follow the son and keep reminding him how wrong the son's behavior is or that the son should come home. It is so tempting to call or text wayward children to remind them that we're waiting for them to come to their senses. Yet, that will only serve to alienate the children.

The wisdom of letting go is both scriptural and necessary. One of the Mother Goose rhymes I used to read to our children says,

> "Little Bo Peep lost her sheep
> And doesn't know where to find them.
> Leave them alone
> And they'll come home,
> Wagging their tails behind them."

It is so hard to leave them alone, to have the faith that they will, indeed, come without our hounding or dragging them home. We must be ready for the possibility that they won't come home, as the father in the Prodigal Son was, and let them go anyway. The father didn't give up hoping, nor did he say, "Fine. But if you go, don't come back." Or "If you want to go, go. When you're ready to repent, I'll take you back, but not while you are still sinning."

The story continues. The son runs into trouble, as all of our children will when they rebel and leave.

"After he had spent everything, there was a severe famine in that whole country, and he began to be in need. So he went and hired himself out to a citizen of that country, who sent him to his fields to feed pigs. He longed to fill his stomach with the pods that the pigs were eating, but no one gave him anything. When he came to his senses, he said, 'How many of my father's hired men have food to spare, and here I am starving to death! I will set out and go back to my father and say to him: Father, I have sinned against heaven and against you. I am no longer worthy to be called your son; make me like one of your hired men.'" (Lk. 15:14-19)

"After he had spent everything." Everything. That is not only money, but also emotional resources, spiritual resources, everything. If the parents have been nurturing (putting the welfare of their child before themselves) when a child cuts himself off from them, he cuts off his emotional as well as financial support. We are not told how much money the prodigal was given or how long it took him to spend it all. We know that he did not go home immediately after the money was gone. He had other resources. He hired himself out. But in leaving, he cut himself off from his emotional resources too. It was not until he had spent everything that he was willing to humble himself and admit he was wrong.

The father could have followed him out into the world, reminding him that he could come home, reminding him he had made a bad decision and had hurt his family. If he had, the son would probably have resented it. No, the father had to let the boy go out on his own. And the son could not return until he could see his own need. How long does that take? Sometimes it takes a very long time. For some, the children will not return to their roots and the basis of their upbringing until after their parents have passed away. But God promises, "Train a child in the way he should go, and when he is old he will not turn from it." (Prov. 22:6)

The son in this story completely humbled himself before his father. It might happen that way, but probably not. It is hard for us to humble ourselves before God. For most people, it's even harder to humble themselves before others, especially their parents. In part that is because of the uncertainty. You see, we are imperfect parents and our children may not be certain we will react like the father in the parable of the prodigal son. So, don't expect your children to come back on their knees. Yet, once they have known the peace and love and forgiveness, and all the other elements of living in a house where God abides, they will eventually see the world outside is jaded and filled with pleasure, but devoid of meaning or peace.

How does the father in the parable react when the son returns? "So he got up and went to his father. But while he was still a long way off, his father saw him and was filled with compassion for him; he ran to his son, threw his arms around him and kissed him." (Lk. 15:20)

The father was looking out for his son before the son returned. He ran out to meet him, to hug and kiss him before he knew the son was repentant. The father was faithful to the son even when the son was not faithful to the father. We must be faithful when our children are unfaithful. We must look for our children who are out in the world and pray for them and, if they will have anything to do with us, welcome them back.

God has given us those children as surely as He has given us our spouses. They can divorce us, but we cannot divorce them. If they are willing to live with us, to put their sin aside while they are with us, we are to be like the father in the Prodigal Son and welcome them, even if they have only come for a brief visit. When the Prodigal Son returned and the father ran out to meet him, the father did not know if the son was staying or if he was forsaking his evil ways for good. He did not make the son feel guilty by telling him how the father had suffered as a result of the son's leaving. Nor did he demand that the son repent before he threw his arms around him and kissed him. That is our Father's unconditional love.

But what of those children who come back for a while and leave again to a sinful life? The father had given his son his inheritance. There was nothing more to give him. If the son had left again, he would have done so with no financial resources. The father would not enable him a second time.

What of the child who lies, is truly sorry for a time, but then lies again? Peter asked the same question. "Then Peter came to Jesus and asked, "Lord, how many times shall I forgive my brother when he sins against me? Up to seven times?" Jesus answered, "I tell you, not seven times, but seventy times seven times." (Matt. 18:21-22)

God not only tells us to forgive so many times, He shows us that no matter how we or our children stumble and fall, fall away from Him, He will always be there, watching for us, waiting to take us back, just like the father in the Prodigal Son.

The book of Judges shows us God's same unfailing love through the recurring cycle that begins and ends with the children of Israel doing evil in the sight of the Lord. (Judg. 2:11, 3:7&12, 4:1, 6:1, 10:6, 13:1.) When they turned away from Him, He did as the father did in the Prodigal Son. He removed His hedge of protection and allowed the evil of the world to overcome His children. Yet, each time they called out to Him, they found God was never far away, ready to replace the hedge of protection and welcome them home. It is the same message as the Prodigal Son, the same description as in Abraham's life, and the same command Jesus gave Peter.

If our children know we love them no matter what, they will someday come back. I know this from Scripture and from my own life. Between my husband and me, we have five adult children. The four older children have been victims of divorce and have grown up with absent parents. All have chosen to follow their own paths rather than the path my husband and I know is God's way. They know our beliefs and they know we live according to those beliefs. They also know how we feel about their life choices and that no matter how much we may disapprove, we will love them. They know that they can call upon us, even as we can call upon our Father. Despite our condemnation of their behavior, three of the four adult children have sought a relationship with us. No, none of them know Jesus yet, but they no longer get angry when we talk about Him. They may not agree, but they listen. They have not closed the door on God because we have not closed the door on them.

As God's children, we know we are loved unconditionally, as Paul wrote, "For I am convinced that neither death nor life, neither angels nor demons, neither the present nor the future, nor any powers, neither height nor depth, nor anything else in all creation, will be able to separate us from the love of God that is in Christ Jesus our Lord." (Rom. 8:38-39) We are merely human, so as parents we often fail. Yet, our goal is to love our children as our Father loves us, unconditionally and to make sure they know they are loved.

CHAPTER 7

Unselfish Love

John 3:16 — For God so loved the world, that He gave His only begotten Son, that whoever believes in Him should not perish, but have eternal life.

There are many who don't know the difference between unconditional love and unselfish love. The difference is great because unconditional love is a love regardless of the response of the person loved. Unselfish love, on the other hand, is a love that puts the other person's happiness or well being first even at great cost. Unselfish love is the next block in building trust. There are not many examples of unselfish love in the people of the Bible. This tells us that it is a rare quality, foreign to our human nature. For example, does anyone doubt that David loved Bathsheba? Yet, had he really loved her with unselfish love, though he desired her, he would have left her alone. She was married when he called her to his castle. (2Sam. 11:1-4)

Had Jacob loved his son Joseph unselfishly, he would have hidden his favoritism instead of flaunting it in Joseph's brothers' faces with a special coat. (Gen. 37:3) His brothers hated him for that coat. Joseph was a dreamer and had problems enough with his brothers without Jacob showing them that he loved Joseph more than he loved them. (Gen. 37:5-11) Any parent of more than one child who shows his favoritism of one over the others shows the same selfish love as Jacob did. It is a love that leaves the other children feeling left out and unloved. I know because my parents made no secret of their favoritism. My sister was my father's favorite. My brother was my mother's. I grew up feeling unloved and unworthy.

Selfish love is what we encounter most often. A classic joke involves the selfishness of a man who buys for his wife a new hammer for her birthday. As a male friend pointed out, it is just as selfish for her to buy him a hammer with the intent that it would get him to work on her "honey do" list.

Roy Croft penned a poem on love that I love. It is a fairly long poem that begins,

> "I love you
> Not only for what you are,
> But for what I am
> When I am with you."
> (Best Love Poems of the American People, selected
> by Hazel Felleman, Garden City, New York: Garden
> City Books, 1960, pp. 25-26)).

The entire poem elaborates on this message, that the source of the poet's love was the change she had made in his life. Until I had a better understanding of God's love, I thought this poem was both wonderful and the best expression of what love should be. It is natural to love those who are good to us and those who help us be better than we are. As Jesus said, "If you love those who love you, what credit is that to you? Even 'sinners' love those who love them." (Lk. 6:32) Through two marriages, I loved my husbands in that way. My love was based on what the relationships did for me, not what I contributed the relationships. That was selfish love. Unselfish love does not ask, "What am I getting out of this?"

It is wrong for a man to love a beautiful woman only because of how he feels and how others look at him when she is around, or for her to love him because of what he can provide. It is wrong for a parent to love a child because of the praise reflected on the parent by a child's accomplishments. It is wrong to love a child because of the love and recognition the child gives the parent. And it is wrong to love a young child for the sense of power and control over the child the parent has.

Many parents, like Jacob, love unconditionally but selfishly. I knew a man and his son who both liked to play golf. To celebrate his son's graduation from college, the father took his son to play golf in Scotland, where the game originated. On the day they were to play the weather was miserable. It was cold, windy and raining. The son wanted to stop. The father should have said something like, "You're right. The weather is awful. Let's go in." But he didn't; he made them press on. While it is important to press on and persevere in some situations, a golf game celebrating the son's graduation when the son wanted to quit hardly seems the time to teach a lesson of perseverance. The father's need to impose his will over his son and for them to complete the father's plan for the day is an example of selfish love.

Unselfish love is Spirit led love, or *Agape*, and transcends our human limits of love. It is God, Himself, who teaches us how to love completely, unselfishly. Whether people know it or not, their capacity to love is from God. As Paul wrote, "Now about brotherly love we do not need to write to you, for you yourselves have been taught by God to love each other." (1Ths. 4:9) We can recognize both selfish and unselfish love through Paul's words to the church in Corinth. "Love is patient, love is kind. It does not envy, it does not boast, it is not proud. It is not rude, it is not self-seeking, it is not easily angered, it keeps no record of wrongs. Love does not delight in evil but rejoices with the truth. It always protects, always trusts, always hopes, always perseveres." (1Cor. 13:4-7)

Indeed, Paul's life serves as a biblical example of unselfish love. We read in Acts 9 and 13-28 of Paul's missionary journeys and of his being driven from cities, beaten and imprisoned repeatedly. He describes his hardships in 2Cor. 11:23-30. One might ask why he continued to travel and preach with these persecutions and hardships. Paul himself provides the answer, a picture of his unselfish love for the unsaved, "I am torn between the two: I desire to depart and be with Christ, which is better by far; but it is more necessary for you that I remain in the body." (Phil. 1:23-24) If his love were selfish, he would have given up. He would let himself be captured and put to death as quickly as possible, for he knew heaven was waiting for him. Instead, he endured the beatings, the narrow escapes and imprisonment because, as he says, "It is more necessary for you that I remain in the body." That is unselfish love.

In Romans 9:1-5 Paul mourns for his unsaved kinsmen, the unsaved Jews. He goes so far as to say, "For I could wish that I myself were cursed and cut off from Christ for the sake of my brothers, those of my own race, the people of Israel. " (Rom. 9:3-4) He would give up his own salvation in exchange for saving all the Jews. It is a truly unselfish, sacrificial love that would even consider trading one's salvation for the salvation of his loved ones.

To find a parental example of unselfish love in the bible, we turn to Job. Job was a very wealthy man, "and he owned seven thousand sheep, three thousand camels, five hundred yoke of oxen and five hundred donkeys, and had a large number of servants. He was the greatest man among all the people of the East." (Job 1:3)

He was also a good father, a loving, unselfish father of grown children, seven sons and three daughters. There probably wasn't the jealously among Job's children as there was among Jacob's because the sons took turns holding feasts for their brothers and sisters. (Job 1:4) Job serves as an example, especially for those of us with children who are off on their own. Our children go off and party, just as Job's did. When a period of feasting had run its course, Job would send and have them purified. Early in the morning he would sacrifice a burnt offering for each of them, thinking, "Perhaps my children have sinned and cursed God in their hearts." This was Job's regular custom. (Job 1:5)

We are not told that Job confronted or condemned his children's partying. As adults, they were answerable to God, not to their father, for their behavior. Yet, as their father, he interceded for them. Job consecrated them and then offered sacrifices on behalf of each child.

Unselfish love is sacrificial love. The greatest Biblical example of unselfish, sacrificial love is our Father's unselfish love for us. He gave us the Law to lead us to Christ (Gal. 3:20). Then He gave us His Son. "For God so loved the world that He gave His one and only Son, that whoever believes in Him shall not perish but have eternal life." (Jn. 3:16) He gave us His Son, so that we may be justified by our faith in Him. (Gal 2:16)

Parents today cannot, as Job did, sacrifice animals on behalf of our children. God doesn't want that type of sacrifice anyway. (Is. 1:11, Jer. 6:20) But we can offer sacrifices of prayer. As David wrote, "May my prayer be set before You like incense; may the lifting up of my hands be like the evening sacrifice." (Ps. 141:2) When we pray for our children, we release them to God's care and control, freeing us to love them, even as sinners, rather than trying to control them. That way God has the power and glory, not us. That is unselfish love. Our children understand unselfish love when they see us give up something precious to us for their benefit alone. Our sacrifices of prayer are to the Lord and our children may not see them as sacrifices.

We have other things we can sacrifice for our children that they will understand, the least of which is money. Unless the parents are barely able to feed and clothe the family, children do not see or understand that money spent on them means money not spent elsewhere. The sacrifice of time, on the other hand, is something children can understand, though even that is sometimes difficult for them to see. From time to time, I had to point out to our younger son that I was giving up time that I might spend otherwise in order to take him somewhere or help him do something. Once I pointed it out, he appreciated the time I gave him.

It is not easy in our culture to make time to listen to a child read or go to recitals or games. We live very busy lives between shuttling kids places and doing errands and going to work, serving on committees, and taking part in bible studies or pursuing other activities that interest our own selves. We are so busy that it is easy to give the children the impression that they are not important.

The easiest and also, perhaps, the most appreciated way we imperfect parents can demonstrate our unselfish love for our children is to listen. Again, we turn to God for our example. "Then you will call upon Me and come and pray to Me, and I will listen to you. You will seek Me and find Me when you seek Me with all your heart." (Jer. 29:12-13) "The righteous cry out, and the Lord hears them." (Ps. 34:17, Prov. 15:29) "The Lord hears the needy and does not despise His captive people." (Ps. 69:33) God listens to us.

As Eliphaz counseled Job, "You will pray to Him, and He will hear you, and you will fulfill your vows" (Job 22:27). Through Isaiah, God said, "Before they call I will answer; while they are still speaking I will hear" (Isa. 65:24). And through Jeremiah, He told us "For I know the plans I have for you," declares the Lord, "plans to prosper you and not to harm you, plans to give you hope and a future. Then you will call upon Me and come and pray to Me, and I will listen to you." (Jer. 29:11-12) "But as for me, I watch in hope for the Lord, I wait for God my Savior; my God will hear me." (Micah 7:7) Our children need to know that we hear them, with the same certainty Micah had; they must know that when they need us, we will act on what they need.

We need to listen to our children and give them our time and attention. Children know if we are really listening or if we are just pretending. We learn who our children are and what their needs are by watching and listening to them. Parents who don't take the time to pay attention to what their children are doing, what they are watching and don't listen to what they are saying don't know their children. Those children cannot be expected to trust that their parents have their best interests at heart.

We live in a busy world where we are bombarded by the noises of radios, smart phones, TVs, constant jabber and the stress of trying to get too much done in too little time. To function in such a world we often block out the noise. It takes a conscious effort to stop and give a child our complete attention, putting the child first. At such times, the child will sense his parent loves him unselfishly. The child will learn to trust those parents and, in turn, listen to them, just as we trust and listen to our Father who listens to our prayers.

I trust God and will obey Him because I know His love for me is unconditional and unselfish. God has demonstrated His unselfish love for me and continues to do so on a daily basis. I know He listens and hears my prayers because He answers them. This is one thing we can learn from our Father and can do. We can give our children our full attention and really listen.

The other chapters of this book show us concrete ways, in addition to prayer and listening attentively, that our Father shows us he loves us, ways we can adopt as we raise our children.

CHAPTER 8

Providing for Needs

*Matt. 6:8 Your Father knows what
you need before you ask Him*

As human beings, we have emotional, spiritual, intellectual and physical needs. We need to be loved. We need to know God. We need knowledge and wisdom as well as physical needs. God satisfies it all, as we are to do for our children with God's help. Because we are needy people, it is such a comfort to us that Jesus tells us in this chapter's verse that God knows what we need even before we ask.

Our first and greatest need is emotional. That is, we all need to be loved. We have seen how He fulfills the need to be loved in the last two chapters. God not only loves us unconditionally and unselfishly, He knows all of our needs. As He provides for those needs, we learn to trust Him more. As we take time to listen to and observe our children, we learn what they need too, often before they ask. As we provide for their needs, their trust will grow. Our children will grow to trust us as we trust God.

Our spiritual need comes from our innate longing to look beyond this life. Except for the relatively few people who have deceived themselves into thinking God is a figment of man's imagination; people inherently know there is something greater than themselves out there. "The heavens declare the glory of God; the skies proclaim

49

the work of His hands." (Ps. 19:1) This inbred awareness of God explains why there are so many religions. Each group is trying to explain the wonders that go beyond man's imagination. Many groups worship the works of God's hands, the mountains, the sun, animals, for example. Some, like the Greeks, have invented gods very much like humans with super powers. All of the religions try to satisfy that spiritual need in each of us.

Only the God of the Bible can do that because He was not invented by men. He revealed Himself, as is described in the Bible. God used individual men to write His Testimony and our history. Men wrote it, but what they wrote was God's words. "All Scripture is God-breathed and is useful for teaching, rebuking, correcting and training in righteousness." (2Tim. 3:16) God satisfies our spiritual need by revealing Himself to us through His Word. He also tells us about ourselves. The Bible tells us how we are created, what our purpose is and what our future will be.

We can satisfy our children's spiritual needs by introducing them to God. When we make God the head of our households and part of our conversation, we open the door for God to fill their needs too. Making Bible study, church attendance and prayer part of family life show our children that we have spiritual needs and this is how God fills them.

I know people who think only fools can believe in God. They quote Marx, "Religion is the opium of the masses." They think faith and intelligence are opposites. Part of the difficulty is in misunderstanding what the Bible is and why God gave it to us. Skeptics do not realize the Bible was never meant to be an all-inclusive textbook of the history of the world. Instead, it is all we need to know for our spiritual journey. It is a road map for getting from here to eternity with Him. The Bible tells us what we need to know about God and about ourselves.

As time has gone by, God has allowed man to learn more and more about how He made the world and everything in it. The fault is not in how much they know, for knowledge is good. The more we know, the more we can use it for God's glory. For example, the more we know of the universe, the more we realize we don't know. The bible has never been disproved.

Science and Biblical Theology are not incompatible. A dear friend of mine, a professor of Theoretical Astrophysics, is a devoted follower of Christ. While teaching at Pennsylvania State University, he held prayer meetings in his office at the beginning of each school day. I recently asked him about the discovery of the so-called, "God particle". He said the standard name is the "Higgs Particle". He said that it was the most important discovery in particle physics in decades and it's discovery shows God's creation to be more elegant than we had thought.

God satisfies our intellectual needs by allowing us to pursue factual revelations beyond the bible, according to each person's abilities and interests. While people have differing intellectual abilities and interests, we all need wisdom.

Unfortunately, many of our nation's most highly educated people do not distinguish between knowledge and wisdom. They elevate knowledge to the place of God, when what they really need wisdom. Knowledge having the answers to the questions, "How". "What?" "When?" and "Why?" It is the study of things. Even in Sociology and Psychology, which study human behavior, people and their behaviors are reduced to numbers.

Wisdom and understanding is seeing the world through God's eyes. There are over two hundred verses in the bible about wisdom. Often wisdom and knowledge are tied together. Knowledge without wisdom is meaningless because wisdom is the ability to understand the world in context. While we can seek knowledge on our own, wisdom comes from God. "To God belong wisdom and power; counsel and understanding are His." (Job 12:13) "For the Lord gives wisdom, and from His mouth come knowledge and understanding." (Prov. 2:6) And God will provide wisdom for all those who seek Him. "If any of you lacks wisdom, he should ask of God, who gives generously to all without finding fault, and it will be given to him."

(James 1:5) "To the man who pleases Him, God gives wisdom, knowledge and happiness." (Eccl. 2:26) We are told a half dozen times in Job, Psalms and Proverbs that the fear of the Lord is the beginning of wisdom. So we must begin with humble worship.

It is hard for people to humble themselves. Yet, that is our only path to true wisdom. "Do you listen in on God's council? Do you limit wisdom to yourself?" (Job 15:8) Not humbling ourselves and asking God for His wisdom is the real foolishness. "Therefore once more I will astound these people with wonder upon wonder; the wisdom of the wise will perish, the intelligence of the intelligent will vanish." (Isa. 29:14)

We can provide for our children's need for knowledge. A home environment that encourages study and honest discussion, good schools, conscientious teachers all provide for our children's intellectual needs. However, the fulfillment of our need for wisdom, like the fulfillment of our need for spirituality, also comes from God. We cannot provide them for our children ourselves. We can only lead them to the Source. When our children see us displaying wisdom and wonder how we understand so much, we can tell them our source of wisdom and pray with them and lead them in bible study.

We also have physical needs. God not only knows our needs, He will meet them, as Jesus assured us, "So do not worry, saying, 'What shall we eat?' or 'What shall we drink?' or 'What shall we wear?' For the pagans run after all these things, and your heavenly Father knows that you need them. But seek first his kingdom and his righteousness, and all these things will be given to you as well." (Matt. 6:31-33)

And a short while later Jesus says, "Which of you, if his son asks for bread, will give him a stone? Or if he asks for a fish, will give him a snake? If you, then, though you are evil, know how to give good gifts to your children, how much more will your Father in heaven give good gifts to those who ask Him!" (Matt. 7:9-11)

Jesus was reminding us what God had already proven throughout the Old Testament. When the Israelites were wandering in the desert for forty years, He gave them manna and quail and water. (Ex. 16:1-17:6) He made their clothes and shoes not wear out in forty years. (Deut. 8:3-4) When they were in the Promised Land, He was the source of their bounty and well being. God told the Israelites He would bring the rain when they needed it and bless their efforts in everything they did if they would love Him with all their hearts. (Deut. 7:12-26, 28:1-14) He told them that because He knew they might think the good rains and freedom from diseases were a matter of luck or that their increase in livestock and agriculture was from their own skill.

It is important for us to know that it is not out of our own cleverness or strength or skill our needs are provided, but that God has provided us with the talents and opportunities. He is in control. He is the provider. It is just as important for our children to know they have the food and clothing and shelter and all their other needs taken care of, because we their parents, are modeling God and providing for them.

Until our very existence is threatened, we adults often don't really believe God's promise to provide for our physical needs. Most of us have much more than our basic needs. We take for granted that our needs will be met and have elevated what we want to what we think we need, such as thinking we need a second car, or cable TV or the newest cell phone, or whatever.

Teaching us to distinguish between wants and needs is an important lesson God teaches us. And like God, we must teach our children to distinguish between their wants and needs and show them that we will fill all of their needs, but not all of their wants. Children, like adults, get to be spoiled brats when they get everything they want.

As we go about our daily lives with our basic needs more than fulfilled, we tend to think we have what we have because of our own efforts, our jobs and our investments. We think we have earned and deserve them. But that isn't true. We have the abilities we do and the jobs we have because God gave them to us. As God said, "I have filled him with the Spirit of God, with skill, ability and knowledge in all kinds of crafts." (Ex. 31:3) It is He who is supplying our needs.

God will not give us everything we want because, as children of this world, our will is often far from God's will and the wishes of our hearts are not what God knows we need.

We can see how God provides as we look at several years of one of my friend's life. God taught her the difference between needs and wants as she learned to trust that He would provide her needs. As her world fell apart and she struggled on her own, she failed and failed again. Our children will also stumble and fail. We must be there for them when they do, just as God was ever faithful to provide my friend's needs.

When I met her, my friend was a widow and lived in an apartment with her daughter. She had a well paying, responsible job. Soon after I met her, they moved into a house to help care for her ailing Christian mother. My friend was devastated when her mother died. While she knew God had taken her mother to a better place and ended her suffering, my friend did not see God working in her own life. He was there to comfort her and guide her without her mother, but she did not know to turn to Him. Likewise, when our children suffer disappointments, we must be there to comfort them, and they must know to turn to us.

Soon after her mother died, my friend lost her job. Without a job, she was unable to pay the rent on the house. She reached the bottom of the barrel, no job, no home. She finally turned to God, and God was always there. God led her to new work, a place to stay, and friends to help her. She shared a house with her niece and began working through a temp agency. A friend gave her a car. Another friend bought medicine she couldn't afford. She was in a church that supported her with prayers and fellowship. While she was grateful to the friends, she knew it was God who had brought these people into her life and burdened their hearts for her and her daughter.

God built her trust by being there as she lost everything she treasured but her daughter. She learned she could do without many of the things she once thought she needed. When she turned to God, He provided, as Jesus promised, food, drink, shelter, clothes, friends to support her. She knows she has a safety net. God will not forget or forsake her.

We are to be our children's safety net. We must provide their food, clothing, shelter, but that is not all. God also has always provided for His children by putting people into their lives to lead and help them, just as He did when He sent Moses and Aaron and Miriam to lead the Israelites out of Egypt and through the desert to the Promised Land. (Micah 6:4) The Israelites could not leave Egypt on their own or even face God themselves when He came to them at the mountain. They said to Moses, "Speak to us yourself and we will listen. But do not have God speak to us or we will die." (Ex. 20:18-19) After Moses died, God raised up Joshua and judges and prophets.

As our Father provided for the Israelites and provides for us by bringing people into our lives, we provide for our children through others. By sending our children to school and enrolling them in sports teams and any sort of lessons, we are bringing people into their lives to guide them in the same way God brought Moses, Aaron and Miriam into the Israelite's lives. We must be careful to send them to people who provide environments that foster our children's academic, emotional, and spiritual growth. We are to closely scrutinize our children's teachers and coaches and teammates, for they will either lead our children astray or on Godly paths.

When we permit our children to spend time with other children, we are enabling the children to learn from and to help one another. So we must pay special attention to our children's friends. When we bring other children into our children's lives, we must provide a place for them to interact free from the temptations of the world. It is not good to leave them without a chaperone for long periods or allow them to participate in activities that will lead them away from

God, like allowing swearing or drinking or watching movies the depict bad language, violence and/or sex. The people we allow into our children's lives must help them follow God.

As our Father teaches us, we also must teach our children to distinguish between needs and wants, and we can do this best by example. We cannot over indulge ourselves and expect our children to be other than self-indulgent. If, before them, we acknowledge and thank God for giving us our health and the ability to do our jobs that provide the money for our homes, clothes, food, they will learn to recognize that it is not that they have earned the right to a nice home, clothes and food, etc. any more than we have. We must show our children we know that God has taken care of us and can be trusted to always do so. They will learn that we provide for them as God provides for us, because we love them as God loves us.

While we are going through something difficult, we often do not see God's hand in our lives. We can trust Him by looking back to the hard times in our lives and seeing His presence. As our children go through difficult times, they, too, will feel alone. We can help them remember times God has helped us and times we have helped them. They will learn to trust us as they experience our providing for their needs, even as we trust our Father by experiencing His provision.

CHAPTER 9

Accounting for Limitations

*Rom. 3:23 For all have sinned and
fall short of the glory of God.*

Training a child in the way he should go, Prov. 22:6, has several components. Training, though, starts with accounting for limitations because the goals themselves must be achievable with the appropriate work and help. Even if we know and account for their limitations, we must realize our children will fall short.

When that happens, we must have patience with them and be ready to forgive. As parents, we often have unrealistic expectations of our children. When we give them tasks for which they are unequipped and expect them to do a good job without help, we are telling them they cannot trust us. Often they do not know their own abilities or limitations. They need us to anticipate when they will need help and provide it. The more we encourage them to grow while providing a helping hand when they most need it, the more they will learn to trust us. This is one way our Father has built our trust, by accounting for our limitations. He often asks of us what seems impossible, but supplies what we need when we need it, so we can do as He asked. (Matt. 6:7-8)) And He is patient for us to learn and grow and He is quick to forgive us when we fail.

God has told us to do many things, but they can be summed into one. We are to grow to be ever more like Jesus. (Rom. 8:29) We know that Jesus lived as a sinless example for us to follow. (1Pet. 2:21-22)

In the Gospels we see Jesus' example. Like Jesus, we are to love God with all our heart, mind, soul and strength (Deut. 6:5, Matt. 22:37) and to love our neighbors as ourselves. (Lev. 19:18, Matt. 22:39) We learn how Jesus treated the beggars, the tax collectors, the temple officials, the multitudes, the children, and the Roman centurion. He did not treat them all the same, but He loved them all. He loved and had compassion for those who were despised by everyone else and even for those who persecuted Him. We also learn how He relied on our Father for everything and how He behaved when He was unjustly accused, beaten, humiliated and finally killed.

Many parents have hopelessly high expectations of their children, just as God's commandment to be like Jesus is hopelessly beyond us on our own. The verse for this chapter is Rom. 3:23, "For all have sinned and fall short of the glory of God." God knew we could not measure up. "My people are fools; they do not know me. They are senseless children; they have no understanding. They are skilled in doing evil; they know not how to do good." (Jer. 4:22) As we are, we can't be like Jesus. The apostle John wrote, "If we say that we have no sin, we are deceiving ourselves, and the truth is not in us. (1Jn 1:8) Even an unknown or unintentional sin is still a sin to God. (Lev. 4:2-4, 5:15)

God has given us a hopeless task. He has commanded us to do what we cannot do. Yet, He is our perfect parent. He knew before He created the world that Adam and Eve would rebel against His one command, that they not eat the fruit of the tree of knowledge of good and evil. Before He created the world, He knew us and chose us, sinful though we are. (Eph. 1:4) He knew we could never do what He required of us, not on our own.

Unfortunately, when most parents set hopelessly high standards for their children, they do not recognize that the goals are hopelessly high. When the standards are for class standing or athletic achievement, the parents are using the world's standards. Being the first in one's class or most valuable player invokes praise of men. Those goals, in addition to being unrealistic, are also leading children down the wrong path. While the child may be talented, gifted, or very good, there is only one "Best" in anything. To set a standard for "Best" overlooks the child's limitations. Even when the standard is to *do* his best, not *be the best*, it is not possible all the time. Likewise, when the parents set a standard for unfailing moral excellence without accounting for human imperfection, they are asking more of their children than God asks.

We have two limitations that keep us from doing what God has asked. First, we are sinners and we have sinned. We cannot fellowship with God or call Him our Father while we stand mired in our sin. Coming before Him in that condition, we would be like Isaiah and cry, "Woe is me, for I am ruined because I am a man of unclean lips." (Is. 6:5) Lips, heart, mind, none of us is clean by God's standards. Knowing this would be the way of things before we were created, He provided a way for us to be cleansed. God promised, "For I will forgive their wickedness and will remember their sins no more." (Jer. 31:34) We are assured, "If we confess our sins, He is faithful and just and will forgive us our sins and purify us from all unrighteousness." (1Jn 1:9)

He sent Jesus, His Son, the second part of the Godhead, to shed His blood that those who believe will be cleansed of their sins. (Matt. 26:28) If we stand behind Jesus and His purity, God will not see our sinfulness, but Jesus' righteousness. (Rom. 3:21-22) It is on this basis we can call God our Father.

When we fall short of God's standard, God makes up the difference. When we set standards for our children that are too high, we must make up the difference. If we expect our children to master all the material in school or expect them to be a valuable player on the team, we must be prepared to help them. We can provide a quiet place and time for our children to study and have available research materials. We can help our children. We can also make available academic and sports camps and church youth groups and retreats and summer camps. We can hire tutors and coaches. Still, if our standards are not in line with their abilities, the adjustment must be ours.

We have another limitation. Once we believe, confess our sins and are cleansed, we are still prone to sin, because we live in a sinful world and have a sinful nature. We can't help it. As Paul wrote, "For what I do is not the good I want to do; no, the evil I do not want to do —this I keep on doing. Now if I do what I do not want to do, it is no longer I who do it, but it is sin living in me that does it." (Rom. 7:19-20)

Again, God knew this before He created the world and He provided for it when the third part of the Godhead, the Holy Spirit, was bestowed on all those who believe. (Lk. 11:13) The Holy Spirit is our helper, as Jesus promised. "And I will ask the Father, and He will give you another Counselor to be with you forever —the Spirit of truth. " (Jn. 14:16-17) God's Spirit is within us to help us. When we are tempted to stray, He convicts us of our sin and leads us to righteousness. (Jn. 16:8)

Following God's example, we bring teachers and coaches into our children's lives. We help them surround themselves with godly friends. We must be very careful in our choices of their teachers, coaches and friends. The teachers and coaches are to help our children be the best they can be to God's glory, not their own or the team's or the coaches' or the teachers'. Once the children are school age, we rarely choose their friends. Still, we have great influence. We can praise their choices and we have screening power; veto power, if you will. Their friends and a godly environment for them to play in are parts of the support structure we provide. And, of course, we are their teachers, coaches and guides too. All of these work together to provided the guidance and strength and training parallel to the Holy Spirit's work for us.

Our children do not need to grow up alone any more than God has left us alone. Yet, our children often feel alone, especially our older children. They cannot feel our love and do not think we understand or accept them. It is not at all unlike when we cannot feel God's presence in our lives because we have shut Him out. No matter how much we shut out God and then feel alone, no matter how much our children shut us out and then feel alone, our love for them must be as apparent as God's love for us. We are to be faithful to them, even when they are not faithful to us.

In the bible, few human parents seem to know the limitations of their children. Most are like Samuel. Samuel was a man of God from the time he was born and was brought to Eli, the priest at the temple, to grow up. (1Sam. 1-3) When Samuel's sons were grown, they turned aside from God's ways, "after dishonest gain and took bribes and perverted justice." (1Sam. 8:3) Yet Samuel sent them out to be judges over Israel. He did not account for their limitations and sent them to do a job they could not do because they were and did evil.

Unfortunately, parents have not changed very much since bible times. When modern parents look at their children, they tend to see what they expect or want to see. Their expectations are often not based on a realistic knowledge of the child's abilities and limitations. Most parents either expect too much or too little from their children.

We can see this in every realm of a child's life. Take sports. Both types of parents vexed my husband when he was a Little League coach of boys between the ages of 9 and 12. All of the boys had been evaluated for their skill levels before being placed on teams. The boys who were skilled beyond their years were placed in a different league. So the boys my husband coached were in the middle and lower end of the skill level. Some parents thought their sons were going to be the next star, if only the coach would give him the chance to shine every game. They would shout criticism from the stands when their son made a mistake. They would either yell at their son and humiliate him in front of the other parents and his team mates, or yell at the umpires or coaches for what the parent thought was a bad call or bad decision. That, too, was humiliating for their son and gave him an example of blaming others for his mistakes.

Other parents underestimated their sons. There was one mother, in particular, who worried and fretted to everyone who would listen that the warm-up and conditioning exercises were going to be too much for her son. She wanted him to be excused. Those exercises were for the boys' good, like God's commandments for us are for our own good. (Deut. 10:13)

We must understand our children's limits and call them to account when they fail, if what we asked was within their limits. The key is in understanding their limitations. God does not overestimate our ability to follow his path. When we fail and make mistakes, He is quick to forgive without letting us off the hook for the responsibility of our own actions. He wants us to take ownership of our shortcomings in order to confess our sins and not blame others, although blaming others is a natural tendency, as when He confronted Adam and Eve in the garden. Adam blamed Eve and Eve blamed the serpent. (Gen. 3:12-13) God wouldn't accept their excuses. He executed the punishment He had promised would be theirs if they disobeyed. (Gen. 3:14-19)

Our Father does not over or under estimate our ability to follow Him. When we fail by being impatient, envious, etc., He does not make excuses for us, but calls us to account by requiring us to confess our sins. (1Jn. 1:9) When our children stumble and fall short, they need to recognize how and why they have failed, and learn where to turn for help.

We see these parents who do not know or accept their children's limitations in academics too. There are those who constantly push, berating a child for grades or honors lower than the parents' expectations or endlessly arguing the child's grades with his teachers. There are also those who excuse bad marks earned by laziness or carelessness as an inability of the teachers to teach. My husband and I learned not to accept our son's explanation of not knowing how to do assigned work because the teacher never taught the material. We knew he was sometimes restless and inattentive and that he often didn't pay attention. Our expectations were based on what we knew he could do if he paid attention and what we knew of the teacher.

In music, in social spheres, behavior and choices, in any area of childhood many parents do not know their child's limitations. When we see a girl who is ten or eleven years old wearing make up and clothes suggesting a sexual invitation, we see an example of a parent not accounting for his child's emotional age or maturity by allowing her to venture beyond the limit of what she can or should handle. Peer pressure in our culture will encourage a boy to begin dating and become sexually active without regard to his emotional or spiritual needs or the consequences. Parents who allow their young children free access to the computer or to watch R rated movies are ignoring their child's inability to distinguish reality from fantasy and moral from immoral. Parents who allow their children to play violent video games are encouraging the child to think the only thing that matters is winning, not who gets hurt or killed. I am so thankful that the Lord does not push us beyond what He knows we can handle.

I admit that I often expect more of our children than they are capable. I should not expect our older children who were never taught about God as children to behave as those for whom God was always a part of their lives. I should not expect a sixteen year old to have the maturity of someone twenty or our children when they were in their twenties to have the maturity of someone forty. Such expectations lead me to voice disappointment and disapproval when they weren't warranted. No wonder my children don't have perfect trust in me as we are to have in our Father.

What I am lacking, in large part, is patience. I do not want to wait for them to be like they will be someday. I want them to be like they will be some day now. I don't want to have to remind them over and over of what they should and should not do. I want them to get it, and make it part of their routine behavior after two or three times being told.

God is very patient with us. Because God knows our weaknesses and limitations, He reminds us what we need to do repeatedly. He knows we need to be reminded and that we just don't get things the first or second or even the tenth time we are told.

All parents get frustrated at having to tell their children over and over and over to do such things as look both ways before crossing a street and say, "Please" and "Thank You", and to take their stuff with them when they leave a room or call when they get to their destination. It feels like they will never learn. We feel like they are not listening or don't care, or don't trust us to have their best interests at heart. But that is the way it is with parents and children. Children don't learn with just one telling.

As God's children, we are no different. Throughout the Old and New Testaments, we are told 38 times to love God and 26 times to not mistreat but to love our neighbor or the stranger who lives among us. And God knows He had to tell us so many times because we forget and we don't listen. We must remind our children of what they must do, just as God has reminded us.

God wants us to be like Jesus and not need to be told over and over again. He knew his apostles would turn from Him, because throughout His ministry, those closest to Him didn't understand what He was about. They constantly marveled at His works (Matt. 8:27, 21:20, 22:22; Mk. 6:51, 10:24-26) and Peter even rebuked Jesus when He told Peter of His coming death. (Mk. 8:31-32) Mark says Jesus told the apostles plainly all that was to happen, that Peter was looking through the eyes of the world. As Jesus told Peter he would, Peter denied he knew Jesus three times after Jesus had been taken. Yet, Jesus did not throw up His hands and exclaim, "I told you and told you. You guys will never get it!" He never discouraged them or shut them out because He understood their limitations.

When we find ourselves short on patience with our children, the only solution is to ask the Holy Spirit for His peace. Just as He will supply wisdom for those who ask (James 1:5), He will also supply you with peace.

Forgiveness is comes with understanding our children's limitations. Understanding that we can never measure up on our own, God is quick to forgive us when we admit our sins. (1Jn. 1:9) Because He is quick to forgive us, we are to be quick to forgive our children, whom we also know cannot always do what is right and their best. We cannot say we have taken our children's limitations into account without being ready to forgive them. Over and over throughout the from the book of Exodus through Malachi, the people forgot what God has done for them or had no faith He would continue, and they turned to idols. Time and again He forgave them. Time and again God told them and tells us such things as, "Return to Me and I will return to you." (Mal. 3:7)

We can learn from God how to realistically look at our children's abilities and limitations. He knows us. He listens to us. We must know our children, listen to them and understand their limitations. When they are capable of more, we need to hold them accountable for their shortcomings and when they need help, we should be there to help without condemnation. When they admit their own failures, we must be quick to forgive. None of us will do this all the time, because we are merely human ourselves. As we become better at understanding and accounting for our children's limitations, they will trust us more. We are blessed to have our Father to look to as an example of parenting for which to strive. He is a Father we can trust.

CHAPTER 10

Communicating Instructions and Consequences

ISA 2:3 Many peoples will come and say, "Come, let us go up to the mountain of the Lord, to the house of the God of Jacob. He will teach us his ways, so that we may walk in his paths."

When I went back to college, ten years after finishing my first master's degree, the first course I took was in computer programming. As I learned FORTRAN, my favorite command was the "If-Then-Else" statement. Very simply, it gave the computer directions that if the input was a certain thing, like a 3, the computer was to do something, like add it to the number 7. If the input was any other number, the computer was always to do something else. The instructions told me, if this, then such and such, or if not this, then something else. I liked the statement because it was straight forward and expressed what action was to happen as a result of an earlier event.

Throughout Scripture, at the same time God tells us what He wants us to do, He tells us the consequences of our obeying or disobeying. It is like the If- Then-Else statement in FORTRAN. He tells us that if we obey, then we will reap His blessings. Or else, if we do not obey, we will suffer the consequences of our disobedience.

It is true, particularly in the book of Leviticus, God gives command after command that is punctuated with, "I am the Lord." Forty-nine times in Leviticus. It seems like He's saying, "Because I said so."

As children, we all hated when our parents answered our question of "Why" with "Because I said so." Our children hate it just as much when we say it to them. Yet, God prefaces these commands by reminding the Israelites what He has done for them.

He is the Lord. He has taken care of them, brought them out of slavery and bondage as no human or manmade God could. He loves them and takes care of them. It is on that foundation, as the One whom they can trust, that He gives his commands punctuated by, "I am the Lord." So it is not really like His saying, "Because I said so", but more like He is saying, "Because I have shown that I know what is right and good for you. Remember Who I am." Through Moses, He not only reminds them of what He has done for them, He tells them outright that these commandments are for their own good. (Deut. 10:13) He has the authority to say, "Because I am the Lord" because He has established the trust.

The goal is the same for us with our children, that obedience should be the result of love and trust. Without trust, people are unwilling to do what is required of them without resentment. That is true for adults as well as children. As Jesus said, "If you love Me, you will obey what I command." (Jn. 14:15) We are no different than the Israelites. That we adults do not obey because we do not trust God is as true for us today as it was for the Israelites.

When the Israelites did not enter the Promised Land, God knew it was because they did not trust Him. Moses told the people, "And when the Lord sent you out from Kadesh Barnea, He said, 'Go up and take possession of the land I have given you.' But you rebelled against the command of the Lord your God. You did not trust Him or obey Him." (Deut. 9:23) We obey because we trust the Lord to keep His word.

God does not treat us as I sometimes treat our children when I assume they should know what they need to do without my telling them. When our younger son was in first or second grade and at a friend's house, the first time I came to pick him up he ran the other way. I got very irritated. I had things to do. So I told him, that whenever he did that, he couldn't visit that particular friend for a month, but if he came right away there would be no restriction.

As our Father does for us, I told him both the punishments and rewards, because we all know it is human nature to try to get away with what we know is wrong. People are inherently selfish. "What's in it for me?" It was in his best interest to follow my instructions.

This inherent self-interest is why it is so important to explain consequences beforehand. Adults as well as children need to be able to weigh the costs of disobedience and the value of obeying. As our children were growing up, I would tell them that they should do what was right because it was right (God's reason, If we love Him we will do His commandments), but that they should also do right because it's smart. (self interest) It is never smart to do what we know to be wrong.

We look to how our Father parents us. He established His love and that we can trust Him to have our best interests at heart, to provide for us and to take into account our limitations. So when He lays out His instructions and their consequences, we should accept them, not as a burden, but in happy anticipation of the benefits.

Likewise, it is most important to establish with each of our children as loving and trustworthy before setting down the rules and consequences. Our children, too, must have no doubt that we parents love them unconditionally and unselfishly, that we will provide for them and will take into account their limitations. With that knowledge, a child will accept that his parents' judgment is better than his own. He will trust his parents and believe they have his own best interests at heart. An outgrowth of their love and trust will lead them to submit to their parents' will, even, as Jesus said, "Thy will be done." (Matt. 26:42)

CHAPTER 11

Allowing Freedom of Choice

Gen. 2:16 And the Lord God commanded the man,
—You are free to eat from any tree in the garden

We looked at Gen. 2:17 in the preceding chapter, when we talked of establishing rules and consequences. The emphasis then was on God's articulating His instruction and the consequences: "but you must not eat from the tree of the knowledge of good and evil, for when you eat of it you will surely die." The emphasis in this chapter is on the freedom God gave Adam and Eve. Had God not given Adam and Eve the freedom to choose to do things His way or not, He could have prevented them from ever reaching the tree. God could have put a glass dome over the tree, so they could see it but not touch it. God could have made the fruit very high off the ground and the trunk too slick and straight to climb. Or He could have made the fruit inedible. Or He could have prevented them from eating it in some way I cannot imagine.

He did none of those things, because He wants us to choose to do what is right. As Moses told the Israelites standing at the threshold of the Promised Land, "This day I call heaven and earth as witnesses against you that I have set before you life and death, blessings and curses. Now choose life, so that you and your children may live." (Deut. 30:19)

For many of us, this is the hardest part of parenting because we want our children to choose to do what is right, not just because we require it, but because we also want our children to <u>want</u> to do what is right. We want them to reap the reward of obedience and do not want them to suffer the consequence of bad choices.

There is a vast difference between when a child says, "Sure," and jumps up when reminded to do a chore or when a child complies grumbling and resentfully. We can demand obedience, but God gave each of us free will. Throughout our lives, from the time we are still tiny, we will try to do things our own way.

Toddlers are so cute, but it is at that stage we first start hearing them exclaim, "No!" If you have ever tried to feed a two-year old food he didn't want, you know how rebellious people can be. This age is called the "terrible twos" because children that age aren't reasonable. That is, they are not old enough understand and trust that what the parents says is to help them or to understand the concept of consequences. They cannot think or see beyond their immediate pleasure or pain.

There are all sorts of rules parents make for their children's own good against which the children rebel, especially in elementary and middle school years. These are the years the children have set bedtimes, are told to drink at least three glasses of milk a day, to brush their teeth twice a day, to call home when they get to friends' houses, to wash their hands frequently, and so many other rules. Every one of the rules is for the child's well being, but they rarely accept that. When our younger son was twelve, he was great at extending his bedtime and trying to get away without brushing his teeth. He thought he was clever, but he was only hurting himself. It was he who was tired in the morning and he who had to have cavities repaired. His life would have been so much easier if he had trusted and obeyed us. He suffered because we had given him the choice.

The high school years are when the challenges to our authority and motivation become serious. Few people go through the adolescent years without either openly or secretly defying their parents. I remember sneaking in after curfew and I remember lying about where I had been. Stupid. Stupid. Looking back, I know those rules were for my own good, like the rules we make for our children and the rules our Father makes for us.

Our Father must deal with us in our resistance to His control, even as we must deal with our children's rebellion against our rules. That rebellious spirit never leaves us. It is our sin nature and has been with us ever since Adam and Eve chose to disobey God and eat the forbidden fruit. We are all like the Israelites who, after God had brought them out of Egypt and sustained them for forty years and given them the land, continued through their cycles of rebellion. Time and again they rebelled against God, did what seemed right to themselves, knowing it was not God's way. As described throughout the book of Judges, they did evil in His sight.

After He tells us what is required and what are the consequences, God lets us choose. Choosing wisely means being able to weigh the consequences. Going back to understanding limitations, we cannot expect small children to make abstract decisions or decisions that will affect their lives in the future. Those ideas are beyond their abilities. But we can give our littlest ones practice making choices with little things, like what they will wear that day or which book to have us read to them. The younger the child, the more we need to limit the choices. An open-ended question like, "What do you want to wear today?" can be overwhelming. It is better to limit the choices, "Do you want to wear this or that?"

As children grow older, the types of choices should grow in proportion to their ability to understand the consequences. For example, when our younger son was in middle school and he showed he was able to assess accurately how long it would take to do his homework, he was allowed to choose to play with a friend after school and do homework later, or do his homework first and enjoy family time after dinner. He knew the consequences of leaving the homework and underestimating how long it would take and then get less sleep, because he had to stay up late or get up early to finish the work. When he was older, we gave him the opportunity to not do the work, but he was well aware of the consequences of bad grades and the terrible feeling of going to class unprepared.

While it is clear God gives us the chance to choose right from wrong and we are to give our children that opportunity, the bible also shows us that sometimes it is appropriate to intervene, as God did in Jonah's life.

We are not told what Jonah was doing or what kind of person he was when God spoke to him. God had a job for Jonah, not necessarily unlike a project we might have for one of our children. On the surface, we see that God wanted Jonah to go to that notoriously evil city of Nineveh to warn them of God's coming judgment. God wanted Jonah to tell them they had a chance to repent and stay His judgment.

The book is about God's willingness to save any who turn to him and about His love for Jonah and the lengths God went to reach and teach Jonah. What God called Jonah to do was for the benefit of those in Nineveh, yes, but it was also for Jonah's benefit. Jonah had a hard, judgmental heart when God called him. Jonah felt better than those idolaters in Nineveh because of their cruelty and idolatry in Israel's past.

So God intervened in Jonah's life. Jonah thought he was so clever, taking that ship to Tarshish to flee from God. (Jonah 1:3) Jonah reminds me of little children who hide their eyes and think we can't see them because they can't see us. It is also like our older children when they somehow think they are clever, trying to sneak in after curfew or leaving without doing some chore.

When Jonah left on the ship, God could have essentially just said, "I'll find someone else." He could have struck Jonah dead for his disobedience. Had God stopped him from getting on the ship, God would have taken away Jonah's choice to be obedient or not. God chose to let Jonah take that step of defiance. Still, Jonah needed to learn that God's rules matter, just as our rules need to matter to our children.

God brought Jonah into compliance, albeit unwilling compliance, by nearly sinking the ship and having a great fish swallow him. (Jonah 1:4-2:10) As parents, if we are aware of our children's disobedience in time, we can stop them, as God stopped Jonah. Their behavior must have consequences.

What God wants from us is not merely compliance though. Jesus rebuked the Pharisees for just going through the motions. (Matt. 23:25, Lk. 11:39) Had God only wanted Jonah's compliance and the repentance of the people in Nineveh, the story would have ended after Jonah warned them and they repented. But the story continues.

The last chapter begins with Jonah's anger. He did the Lord's bidding, but not with the heart of compassion God wants in all of us. Jonah complained that it was just as he knew it would be and he would rather be dead than see the people of Nineveh saved. God could have lectured Jonah about the value of each soul. Jonah would probably have tuned God out, just as our children tune out our lectures about the values and perspectives they should have. Instead, God gave Jonah a lesson. He had taught Jonah His power and Jonah's need for obedience in the sea. He also knew of God's forgiveness, because God had forgiven the people of Nineveh when they repented. Now Jonah needed to have his own heart softened.

It was hot and God provided a vine to give Jonah shade. We are told Jonah was very happy about the plant. (Jonah 4:6) Then God provided a worm that chewed and withered the plant, a scorching sun and an east wind. Once again, Jonah said he was so angry he wanted to die. God now had Jonah's attention and the opportunity to get Jonah to see why each of God's children is important to Him.

But the Lord said, "You have been concerned about this vine, though you did not tend it or make it grow. It sprang up overnight and died overnight. But Nineveh has more than a hundred and twenty thousand people who cannot tell their right hand from their left, and many cattle as well. Should I not be concerned about that great city?" (Jonah 4:10-11)

When we are teaching our children life changing lessons, as God was teaching Jonah, we have to first get their attention. It is important in building trust for our children to know that we will intervene when their choices have life long consequences.

We found one of our daughters was failing senior English because she had assignments she had not handed in. Without that course, she would not graduate high school. We intervened. We told her that we had talked to the teacher and found out how many and what assignments were missing. She had the choice to get the work done and in before the end of the semester or fail. She knew that if she failed, she would not graduate with her class. We added that she would be grounded the next semester. Those were consequences she could understand.

She finished the work on time and got a B. She was angry with us for a while, but she knew we had her future in mind. The situation made our relationship stronger. Jonah's experiences taught him to obey as God sustained him in the fish. Our children must also know we will intervene when the choices have life long consequences.

Had her bad choices involved bad company or playing with drugs or alcohol or tobacco, in short, physically damaging or life threatening things, our intervention would have been more dramatic and direct. When our older son was in middle school and got in with some boys who were cutting school and stealing things during lunch, we intervened and gave him the choice to find new friends or face the humiliation of my sitting with him at lunch time to make sure he wasn't with those boys. Yes, he was mad at us, but he complied. He was very grateful he had broken off the friendships when the other boys later got into serious trouble. The friends he subsequently chose have become life long friends.

It is hard to give our children the freedom to choose because being free to choose means being free to fail as well as free to succeed. It means our children are free to disobey, to dash our hopes for them, to trample our trust. We must allow them to be free to experience the consequences, just as our Father has done for us. We must also be ready to step in.

Fortunately, situations that are life threatening or life changing are rare. Building trust requires we will know when to intervene and when to let them go. This requires foreseeing consequences. While we can anticipate simple consequences, most decisions are made with imperfect knowledge. As the saying goes, "Hindsight is 20-20."

Yet, God knows everything. He is ever present and all knowing. The words of Job rings true for us: "To God belong wisdom and power; counsel and understanding are His." (Job 12:13) "Do you listen in on God's council? Do you limit wisdom to yourself?" (Job 15:8)

Our children must be able to count on us to allow them to step out, as the father did in the Prodigal Son and as God did when he let Jonah get on the boat. Only God can grant us the discernment to know when to step back and when to act. They must also be able to count on us in those situations in they need a safety net, just as we know God is our safety net.

CHAPTER 12

Keeping Your Word

*Neh. 9:8 You have kept your promise
because you are righteous.*

We began this book with the Scout Oath, "On my honor I will do my best to do my duty". If the scout lives by this promise, he will be a person of integrity and people will trust him. Being a person of integrity, a person who keeps his word, is fundamental to building trust. The saying, "That man's word is his bond," says much about the person. The old saying, "A man is as good as his word," has always been true. Without a history of keeping one's word, there is no trust. Yet, we live in an age without trust.

We live in an age without trust because the American people have been and are betraying trust all the time. Our acceptance of betrayal is, perhaps, the most condemning mark of our country. The evidence is all around us.

Our country has more lawyers and law suits than any other country. We have tobacco companies who knew their product was both poison and addictive. We have a tire company who knew their tires were unsafe. And we have people who will try to blame others for injuries that were caused by their own misuse of equipment and poor choices. A microwave manufacturer was sued because there was no label warning that putting a cat in the microwave to dry might be damaging to the cat's health. A fan company was sued because when a man stuck his toddler's face in the path of the fan, his son got hurt. When we buy a product, we implicitly promise to take responsibility for how we use it. Or we should.

We were betrayed in government when a former president admitted to having told falsehoods under oath. When the American people didn't rise up in indignation at his flaunting of our constitution, which he had promised under oath to uphold, we showed the world we had lost our moral compass.

We cannot point our fingers at the prominent people without turning that same finger against ourselves. The divorce rate in this country has been about fifty percent since I can remember. The divorce rate is the same in churches as in the general population. When we get married, most of us promise, "For better or for worse, for richer or for poorer, in sickness or in health, until death do us part." As a people, we are poor at keeping our word.

Throughout the bible are many examples of people not keeping their word, Lot's daughters (Gen. 19:1-11), Achan (Josh. 6:18-20, 7:1-23), Delilah (Judges 16). We haven't changed a bit, and neither has the need for keeping our word. It is required for building trust. Always keeping one's word is so basic people often underestimate its importance.

When we tell our children we will do something, whether it is doing something with or for them or rewarding them or punishing them, our word must be our bond and we must keep it. As parents, when it comes to punishments, there are many reasons we don't keep our word. Regardless of the reason, each time we don't, the foundation of trust is damaged. For example, how many times have we heard or said ourselves, "The next time you do that I'm going to..." And the sentence is finished with something neither the parent nor the child believes will happen. Many parents say such things for the shock value. The child knows that if he touches the thing he shouldn't he won't really be grounded for the rest of his life, or that if he doesn't come in immediately his parent won't really lock him out for the night, but the extreme of the verbalized punishment conveys that the parent is upset to the point of being ready to do something about the disobedience.

Such scenarios generally take place after the child has been told what to do or what he could not do several times without result. Often, the parent will escalate both the proposed punishment and the volume of the request each time it gets repeated. Such phrases as, "I mean now" and "If I have to ask you again, you're in trouble" indicate that neither the parent nor the child are ready to stop what they're doing and do something about what's been asked.

Parents would like their children to comply the first time they're told or asked. It would be so much more convenient. Parents don't like to have to get angry to get a response. At the same time, too many parents in our busy world are too busy doing their own thing to take the time to follow through and see to it the child does what he's asked. The child is slow to react because he knows his parent is too busy and that the punishment will never come.

There is a great difference between being long suffering, being patient, and being so busy the consequences are never seen. God is patient and long suffering with us, and we must be eternally thankful for His patience. As Peter says in 2Pet. 3:8-9 "But do not forget this one thing, dear friends: With the Lord a day is like a thousand years, and a thousand years are like a day. The Lord is not slow in keeping his promise, as some understand slowness. He is patient with you, not wanting anyone to perish, but everyone to come to repentance."

We know from fulfilled prophecy and other events throughout the bible, what the Lord says will happen, will happen. Abraham and Sarah did have a child. (Gen.22:17) Isaac and Rebecca waited 20 years to have a child. (Gen. 25:20-26) The Israelites were enslaved in Egypt for 400 years, just as God had foretold Abraham. (Gen.15:13) The Israelites did turn away from God and God dispersed them into the nations, saving forever for Himself a remnant, just as He had foretold to Moses. (Deut. 28:62-68) God did come, our

Messiah clothed as a baby to serve, heal, suffer, die and rise again, all as had been foretold throughout the prophets. None of these things happened immediately after they were foretold. Sometimes hundred of years separated the foretelling and the events. But from our experience, we know that God keeps His word. We know that one day He will return to judge this world and to take His children home.

Another reason parents don't follow through with punishments is that they don't want to see their children suffer. Every parent knows, just as no child can understand, that it really does hurt the parent to discipline a child more than it hurts the child. We don't want our children to miss a birthday party or concert or sporting event. We push back the punishment until it is no longer meaningful or it won't happen at all. But it is important to have consequences that are meaningful to the child and ones the children know the parent will enforce.

The parent must come up with consequences he is willing to administer and consequences that will be important to the child. For example, I was unwilling to pronounce consequences that would have punished others as they punish the offending child. Since our child enjoyed participating in team sports, it might have been a tempting punishment to say he couldn't play the next game. That would have been a bad consequence because it would have taught the wrong lesson: telling a child who is on a team or part of a group project or music ensemble that he must miss the event because of his misbehavior. While it is a punishment the child would understand and would be easy for the parent to enforce, joining a team means making a commitment to others. Regardless of the pleasure the child may get from participating. Thus, the effect of the punishment, his absence, lets down the team.

For children, being committed to God is an abstract concept. Team participation is an excellent way to teach our children commitment in a way they will understand. So holding out participation as a reward or withholding ability to participate as a punishment after the child has already joined a team may sound easy, but is a bad choice of consequences.

I am also unwilling to pronounce consequences that will punish the rest of our family as we punish the offending child. We had one television. Generally, as the children were growing up and in school, lives were too busy for them to watch television during the day. After dinner, we'd all watch television together. I wouldn't give a punishment forbidding the television from going on because it would punish everyone. Instead, we would require the child to spend that time in his/her room while the rest of us enjoyed the show.

It is important that the child know he has control over himself and freedom of choice, but that he doesn't have control over his parent. The time after I'd told our son the consequences of his running away when I picked him up, he ran the other way again. He didn't get to play with that friend for a month. He never again ran away when I came to pick him up. He even warned his friends when they were at our house that when their mother's came to pick them up, they had to go right away. If I had not followed through, his trust in my word would have been destroyed. If the child's behavior determines the parent's behavior, the child has the control. We don't have control over our Father and our children must not have control over us.

Keeping our word does not only involve the discipline we promise. I know a woman whose heart is breaking for her granddaughters because their father doesn't keep his promises to come see the girls and go to their gymnastics events and recitals. Children want their parents to be consistent and do what they said they would do.

Sometimes parents say they will do things they cannot fulfill, knowing they cannot fulfill them. Of these parents, many do that because they really want to do what they have said. "Someday I will take you to...." It is heartbreaking because the parent knows all along it will never happen while the child tries to believe the parent. The child will feel cheated when it doesn't happen, not so much because the trip wasn't taken, but because the parent didn't keep his word. Betrayal of trust is a far greater pain than losing a privilege.

Some make promises they can't fulfill, hoping they will be able to keep them or thinking they can fulfill them. To avoid the sense of betrayal, the parent should preface the promise with something like, "If I have time when I finish this, I'll do that with you." Or, "If we can afford it...," Or, "If Dad can get the time off...". When the qualifiers are explained, the parent still must try his best to make sure the thing promised happens, so the child sees that the parent tried to make it happen. Then, if the event doesn't happen, the child will probably be disappointed, but he won't feel betrayed.

Often parents make empty promises to brush off the child. They convince themselves they don't have to deal with the child now because the child has been promised something later. It placates the child until the child realizes it isn't going to happen. This causes the child to become resentful.

Part of the scout oath with which we began this book says that the scout promises to be trustworthy. As we are trustworthy, our children will learn to be trustworthy. Being trustworthy has a price. Keeping our promises will often be inconvenient and expensive. Keeping our promises takes time, energy, and finances. Keeping promises is part of sacrificial love. Therefore, we cannot make promises of either discipline or rewards that are meaningless or that we cannot or will not keep. We must mean what we say and be willing to follow through, even when it's inconvenient, even when it hurts or is expensive.

Our children grew up on Dr. Seuss. One of our favorite books was <u>Horton Hatches the Egg</u>. (Random House, 1940) In this book, Horton, an elephant, promises to sit on Mayzie bird's egg until she returns. Despite all the terrible things that happen to him, Horton keeps repeating, "I meant what I said and I said what I meant. An elephant's faithful 100%."

We have to be like Horton. We must say what we mean and mean what we say. That is part of what becoming like Christ means.

Nancy C. Gaughan

God promised us a Messiah who would die for our sins. Imagine how it hurt Him to send His own Son and watch Him suffer to reconcile us with Himself. We trust God because He keeps His word. Our children will trust us because we keep our word too.

CHAPTER 13

Staying in Control

Prov. 29:11 A fool gives full vent to his anger,
but a wise man keeps himself under control.

This chapter is on the need to stay in control, regardless of the unexpected, as the last step in building trust.

I will never forget going to my first Christian sponsored concert. The theater was crowded and the lights were dimmed as we all waited expectantly for the artist to appear on stage. His introduction heightened our excitement. He stumbled on a stair as he came onto stage amidst great applause. The audience pretended not to notice he has stumbled. He got to center stage and looked around somewhat anxiously. Something was wrong. As he began to speak, we all realized the microphones weren't working. Suddenly his recorded background music began, first too loud, then too slow, then stopped before he could begin his first song. By this time, we were all anxious for him.

At that point, when the unexpected happened, when everything went wrong for the performer, he could have lost control. He could have panicked and simply walked off the stage, or become very angry at the technical crew in charge of the electronics. He knew he was losing his audience. Yet, in a twinkling his anxiety disappeared. He threw his head back and laughed as he exclaimed, "Lord, I'm sure glad You are in control, because I'm certainly not!"

Everyone laughed as the artist reminded us we are children of a Father who is in control and loves us. With that reassurance, our thoughts returned to the concert, which proceeded beautifully. Surely God was in control.

As Paul said, "We know that the law is spiritual; but I am unspiritual, sold as a slave to sin. I do not understand what I do. For what I want to do I do not do, but what I hate I do. And if I do what I do not want to do, I agree that the law is good. As it is, it is no longer I myself who do it, but it is sin living in me. I know that nothing good lives in me, that is, in my sinful nature. For I have the desire to do what is good, but I cannot carry it out. For what I do is not the good I want to do; no, the evil I do not want to do —this I keep on doing." (Rom. 7:14-19) That describes our sin nature, and everyone has one, including our children.

There are many things we can do when confronted with a rebellious spirit in our children. The worst reaction we can have is to not deal with the rebellion. We can avoid dealing with it in two ways. We can just send the child away. In smaller children this can take the form of "Go to you room", although their rooms should not be places of punishment, but of refuge. Or we can say, "Go play with so-and-so, or "Go outside." Older children are sometimes just told to leave.

It is the worst reaction because it does the most to destroy our children's trust in us. When we send them away in anger or frustration, we are telling them that we reject them as well as their behavior. We are telling them our love is conditional.

The other form of not dealing with disobedience is ignoring it. I have seen parents laugh off children openly defying them. The parent might say, "Don't go there," or "Don't do that." When the child does, the parent pretends he doesn't see or doesn't care. By not dealing directly with the disobedience in this way, we prove ourselves to be liars. When we tell them rules and consequences and teach them that the rules are for their own good, then don't hold the children to the consequences, we are saying the rules were not important after all. The next chapter is called, "Keeping Your Word." Following through is an important part of keeping your word.

The second worst reaction we can have to our children's disobedience is the opposite extreme of sending away or ignoring the defiance. Anger is a natural reaction to disappointment, but it is not a wise reaction. It is a reaction that, I confess, I am guilty of too often, acting out in anger. We become angry because our child's disobedience challenges our authority. It is also frustrating to know that what we have required is for the good of the child and, yet, the child is rejecting it. We often react out of anger because when the child is rebellious, we feel he is rejecting us. That may be partially true, but for the most part, he is not rejecting his parent. He is rejecting the sense you have control over his life.

Some people get angry when the children disobey because they fear the reaction of others who see the consequence of the child's disobedience. They see their child's accomplishments and behavior as a reflection on themselves. When the child falls short, the parent sees it as a poor reflection on himself. If the child does not do his homework, he gets bad grades. If he doesn't brush his teeth, he has poor dental health, etc. Not only does the child suffer of his falling short, but also many parents worry what the teachers or dentists or others might think of their parenting.

Even when a child disobeys unintentionally, we sometimes get angry. I sometimes yelled at our younger son because of his carelessness and inattentiveness. He didn't mean not to feed the dog, but he just didn't notice that her bowl was empty, again. He meant to call when he got to his friend's house, but got busy playing and forgot. While it was important our son sees consequences for such behavior, it is also important not to lose my temper.

None of us parents are perfect. Our unconditional, unselfish love is not always apparent. We can't always be with our children to help them. We are sometimes too busy to notice even they need help. The more we fail, the less our children trust us to have their best interests at heart, and the more defiant they will be. At such times, as soon as we recognize our shortcoming, we must admit it to our children and ask forgiveness, telling them what we should have done or said.

Consider our Father. He is perfect. We have no reason not to trust Him. He is always with us. (Josh. 1:5) He has proven His unconditional, unselfish love. Yet we still rebel. We can learn how to best deal with rebellious hearts by seeing how our Father deals with us.

First, He is proactive, not reactive. He knows what we will do. He is ready for our disobedience when we choose wrong. As we discussed in a previous chapter, He tells us what the rules are and what will happen if we do not follow them. For us to do that means we have considered disobedience as a possibility and accounted for it. Disobedience should not take us by surprise.

Too often parents are surprised when their children don't follow their instructions. In their surprise, they strike out in anger. They shout and scream, rant and hit. Some curse. When we have planned for both their obedience and disobedience, we can react calmly.

Unless our will is bent to God's, we will be disobedient. Unless our children's wills are bent to ours, and they rarely are, our children will be disobedient too. We are imperfect and should account for our children being imperfect.

We need to remember God is in control because, despite what our children think, as adults we have no control over much in our lives. Like that artist when the microphones didn't work, things sometimes don't work in our lives, usually unexpectedly. Trusting that our Father is in control enables us to gain control of ourselves, to have peace when others would despair or get angry or panic. Our trust and understanding helps us see any particular situation in which we might find ourselves through God's eyes, with eternal, not just immediate, perspective.

The self-control comes in calling on God's strength and wisdom and claiming His promises. From the time the artist acknowledged God's sovereignty and control, the concert turned around. The audience, sensing that he was not upset, settled down and enjoyed the concert. Whether or not the microphones or his background music worked, the artist was able to sing God's praises to an audience who could see God's peace and joy in him, despite all the difficulties.

It must be made clear that getting angry is not the problem. Losing control is. We are to model God and He gets angry, very angry. We are warned in 190 different verses throughout the Bible about God's wrath. Jesus got angry with the Pharisees. (Matt. 15:7, 22:18, 23:25-27, Mk. 7:6, Lk. 12:56, 13:15) Still, it is not uncontrolled anger. He warns us of the rules and the consequences, so we know what we must do. He warns us that He will be very angry if we turn to other gods, yet we cast Him aside repeatedly. He gives us less, not more than we expect or deserve in punishments.

We, too, get angry. When Paul writes the Ephesians what it means to, as he says, put off their old selves, that is, to be conformed to God's image, he cautions them not to let their anger cause them to sin and not to let the sun to go down while they are still angry. (Eph.4:26) He goes on to tell us to get rid of rage, bitterness and malice. (Eph. 4:31) Anger in and of itself is not bad. Uncontrolled anger is. We are to exercise self-control in the midst of our anger.

The kind of anger that leads to rage is sudden, most often short lived, and usually the result of unexpected behavior. People experience what is called "Road Rage" when someone suddenly cuts them off as they drive. I became enraged when our granddaughter refused to let me put drops in her eyes. I was angry because she feared the drops more than she trusted me. I shouted at her how bad she was for not trusting me. I was awful. I should have stopped and prayed. Instead I became very angry.

Rage is not the only way people lose control. They become despairing. Bad news comes. A child dies, a loved one has cancer, or any one of many heartbreaking things. Yet, we need to trust God.

Not only is He in control, He has told us, "Blessed are they who mourn for they shall be comforted" (Matt. 5:4) When all seems hopeless, our hope is in the Lord.

People also panic. Anger, Rage and panic all stem from the same cause, having unrealistic expectations of ourselves, of things we use and of others. We are told we all will experience suffering. Ecclesiastes 3 lists pairs of all the activities we will experience during our lives, including mourning and weeping.

I should have taken into account that my granddaughter was only 7 and would be so afraid of drops that she would not believe me that these drops wouldn't hurt. Husbands and wives will let each other down. Children and parents and friends will fail or fall short. No equipment lasts forever. When we take into account the shortcomings, we are not taken by surprise and enraged or thrown into a panic.

Chapter nine discussed the need to take limitations into account. This chapter is on the need to stay in control as the last step in building trust. When we have done everything right and things still don't work out, we, with the help of the Holy Spirit, must stay in control, just as the performer did, so those around us gain the confidence that is ours.

We are not born with the knowledge or ability that because of God's power and love, we can be at peace in any circumstance. We are not born with self-control. It is a fruit of the Holy Spirit. (Gal. 5:22-23) If you watch any infant or toddler, you will see our first instincts lead us to wail and thrash when we are upset. The littlest things can send a little one into a tantrum. Nor does self-control come as a natural part of aging. There are adults who seem most childlike because they panic easily and throw temper tantrums too. As with any of the fruits, we gain self-control as our faith grows and matures. We need the Holy Spirit to help us, and few master it even with His help. We all panic or lose our tempers from time to time, gradually gaining control as we grow.

We panic and our children panic because we don't remember to turn to God. One day Jesus said to his disciples, "Let's go over to the other side of the lake." So they got into a boat and set out. As they sailed, He fell asleep. A squall came down on the lake, so that the boat was being swamped, and they were in great danger. The disciples went and woke him, saying, "Master, Master, we're going to drown!

He got up and rebuked the wind and the raging waters; the storm subsided, and all was calm. "Where is your faith?" He asked his disciples. In fear and amazement they asked one another, "Who is this? He commands even the winds and the water, and they obey Him." (Lk. 8:22-25)

Where was their faith? Jesus had told them to go out onto the lake. He was with them, so they knew they were in God's will. They were confused and frightened and forgot to turn to God. They only knew they were failing at trying to save themselves and they panicked. They knew from earlier miracles of Jesus that He was of God, even if they did not fully realize He was God. Had they stopped and thought, they would have known God would not let Jesus die in a storm.

Our children often forget to turn to us as well. They panic and cry out of the hopelessness of a situation. When He awakened, Jesus did not first respond to the disciples' panic. He calmly took charge, rebuked the sea, then turned to the apostles and addressed their real problem, lack of faith. When He took control, they all calmed down.

As our children are growing up, we need to be in control of ourselves, so we are able to take control in situations in which they lose control. When they see us in control and we help them gain control, they will learn self-control and learn to trust us even when they can't trust themselves. We must teach them to ask the Holy Spirit for self-control.

Just like the apostles, people today are prone to panic or let their anger get out of control when the unexpected happens. The panic and anger come from being forced to face our unrealistic expectations. We aren't all we thought or hoped we were. We can't handle or do whatever it is.

Self directed panic and anger often turn outward against others as individuals resent and resist the control other people or God has over them. Everybody wants to be his own boss and many get angry when they can't be. In children, this kind of anger is called acting out. People purposely break laws and defy authorities to catch and correct them. We say of these people, "He has a problem with authority." We see it at every age. It is a trap because none of us has control over our lives. Solomon wrote that while man's mind plans his way, it is God who directs his steps. (Prov. 6:19) Life will become easier the sooner we acknowledge God's control and surrender our lives to His will.

The anger also turns outward toward others as people look to others to blame for their own shortcomings. Such anger is often revealed by statements that start with such phrases as "You made me...." No, I didn't make our child spill the soda or break a toy or whatever else I am being accused of. He struck out at me because he was careless or rambunctious and didn't want to admit that it was his fault, that he had failed.

We all know adults who chronically blame others and become very angry for their own failures. This too is a trap. Freedom comes in confessing our shortcomings and turning to God for help. Just as He helped the apostles, He will forgive, guide and help us.

Another cause of uncontrolled anger is in over estimating others' abilities. We dealt with this in Accounting for Limitations. Unrealistic expectations and demands for perfection are doomed to disappointment. Things do not always go as we want. People cut us off on the freeway, people hurt us, things break. If we account for the limitations, we are prepared in times of failure. Unrealistic expectations of parent for their children and the ensuing anger can teach a child that losing control is part of life. It can develop a deep distrust of the parent.

I knew a man whose temper was out of control throughout his life. As a child he was called Rumplestilzkin after the Grimm fairy tale character who had such a terrible temper.

I thought his temper had been caused because he was an older graduate student, living in a dormitory, with nothing and no one to call his own. He finished his Ph.D., got a job, married a woman with two children, and bought a beautiful home. He had an education, a home, a job, a wife, two stepchildren, and finally his own baby to love. I thought his anger would disappear in the happiness of all he had, but the temper tantrums did not stop.

He had unrealistic expectations of all of the children, and when they fell short, he got very angry. They knew he loved them but they could not trust him. When the baby spilled his milk, as babies do, he swore at him. When his daughter left her shoes in the family room and when his older stepson had trouble understanding geometry, he screamed and called them names.

Because they could not trust him, they obeyed him out of fear, not out of love and security. The outburst left scars on the baby.

The man died two weeks after his son turned three. After he died, it was years before the baby stopped suddenly getting sad and remembering, "My Daddy called us names." It shows the effect an out of control parent can have on a child. It is important to stay in control.

Jesus asked the apostles, "Where is your faith?" Where is our faith? We all have storms in our lives. Sometimes the storms are life threatening, as was the apostles' squall. Just as with the non-believing world, we get sick, we get hurt, people we love will disappoint and hurt us. God will not always physically heal us or save us, but He will always be in control and use our suffering for our own good. (Rom. 8:28) Just as Jesus calmed the sea and saved the apostles, God is able to calm the storms for us if we put our faith in Him. He will ultimately bring us home to Him.

In the chapters on Accounting for Limitations and Communicating Instructions and Their Consequences and on

Freedom of Choice, we said we had to acknowledge our children might fall short and be prepared for our children to fail. If we have foreseen this eventuality, we can stay calm to intervene or to allow consequences to take place. Even if we are angry, we can calmly administer the consequences we have previously explained.

As always, we look to God's example. Our sin does not take Him by surprise. He has clearly described to us the consequences of our unrepentant sin. When He comes to judge the earth, we will be without excuse if we have not turned to and trusted Him. As David wrote, "No one whose hope is in You will ever be put to shame, but they will be put to shame who are treacherous without excuse." (Ps. 25:3) When He comes it will be terrible for those who have not put their hope in God. "Wail, for the day of the Lord is near; it will come like destruction from the Almighty. Because of this, all hands will go limp, every man's heart will melt. Terror will seize them, pain and anguish will grip them; they will writhe like a woman in labor. They will look aghast at each other, their faces aflame. See, the day of the Lord is coming a cruel day, with wrath and fierce anger — to make the land desolate and destroy the sinners within it. "(Isa. 13:6-9)

But God will never be out of control. It will all be just as He said it would. And He will save those who put their trust in Him.

We can't work all things for the good for our children, as God does. We do not have that power, but we can stay calm when they panic and stay calm when they defy us. We can prove ourselves trustworthy and we can reassure them and point them to our Father who can and will cause all things to work together for the good. We are to mirror our Father for our children. They will learn to trust us and to trust God when they see us take charge when they are panicked or enraged and see us turn to God when we would have otherwise lost control ourselves. From trust comes love and obedience.

CHAPTER 14

God, The Perfect Parent

*Matt. 5:48 Be perfect, therefore, as
your heavenly Father is perfect*

In this chapter I contrast an example of terrible parenting with
parenting as God parents us.

We learn how to be good parents from our Father. The greatest
gift we can give our children is one we have learned as children from
our Father, the gift of trust. Just as our Father has taught us we can
trust Him, we must teach our children they can trust us. We are
to mirror God. They learn to trust us whom they can see so that
one day they can trust Him whom they can't see. It is easy to trust
and obey God in love because we know He loves us unselfishly and
unconditionally.

I once witnessed an example of the worst of parenting. It serves
as a pointed contrast to how God parents us and encompasses the
points we made in earlier chapters.

I used to own a little convertible that I drove with the top down
even in the hottest summer days in southern Arizona. That was
fine as long as the car was moving. Early one August afternoon, I
was sweltering, stopped at the far end of a row in a warehouse store
parking lot. The lot was packed and I chose to wait for two women
pushing their cart toward a car at my end of the row. With my top

down, I couldn't help overhearing them. They were the mother and grandmother of a little boy about two years old sitting in the cart.

The baby had behaved badly in the store. Their car was quite far from the warehouse, near the end of the row. As they approached it, their complaints and grumbling grew louder and more vehement. They were blaming the warehouse for having long check out lines and blaming each other for shopping past the baby's lunch and nap times. They were so hot and so angry, but they were hardest on the little boy, who cowered in the oversized cart with all the oversized packages.

They grumbled all the while they were unloading the purchases. As they closed the back of their van, they ordered the boy to stand up so they could more easily pick him up to get him into the car. When he refused, they began to yell and swear at him. No promises or threats would get him to stand up in that cart. He cowered there, alternately whimpering and stubbornly pouting. Finally, the grandmother got into the driver's seat and shouted to her daughter to move the cart out of the way and to get in. She yelled, "If he won't stand up, we'll just leave him here."

As the mother started to move the cart, that was all the baby could take. He let out a terrified howl. With the little boy wailing and clutching for her, she pushed the cart out of the way of their car and started to get into the passenger side. The little boy was hysterical, standing, screaming for his mother, who told him it was too late, that he should have stood up earlier. The grandmother backed up just enough for the mother to get out, snatch the baby, and throw him into the back seat. As they pulled out and drove away, I could hear them still screaming at the crying baby. I was horrified and felt sick.

Let's look at the contrasts and be grateful our Father is perfect, beginning with God's character. The fruits of the Spirit define God's character as we can emulate it. "But the fruit of the Spirit is love, joy, peace, patience, kindness, goodness, faithfulness, gentleness and self-control." (Gal. 5:22-23) As God wrote through John, "God is love." (1Jn. 4:8) These women showed no love or patience or kindness or for the boy at all. They had no more self-control than the baby had.

How could a baby learn unconditional love from his mother or grandmother when they threatened to leave him in a parking lot? This example may seem extreme, but I have heard people, both fathers and mothers, threaten to leave children who lagged behind or would not go where the parents were walking. All parents at some time have been in a situation when they have said something like, "Come this way," or "Hurry up, we're in a hurry," or "Come on, it's time to go, NOW." Many of us have been frustrated enough to say, "Fine. Just stay there, I'm leaving." But that is not what God does. He will never leave or forsake us. (Deut. 31:6) And He never threatens to.

In a situation like that, the parent needs to stay in control. When Jonah went the other way, God stopped him until Jonah was willing to go where God wanted. (Jonah 1:3-2:10) Jesus came to find the lost sheep and carry them back. (Lk. 19:10, Jn. 3:17) When our children are disobedient and defiant, they are wandering out of our fold we need to go to the child and listen. We need to find out if the child has a reason besides stubbornness for not going. They sometimes do. In any case, the parent needs to take control.

God's love is unselfish. He gave His son that we might be saved. (Jn. 3:16) In the parking lot, the women's love was both conditional and selfish. Their love was conditional on the baby's behavior. They were angry with the little boy first because he had embarrassed them in the warehouse. Had they had unselfish love, as our Father has for us, they would have made the adjustment to accommodate the baby, like buying lunch, instead of expecting the child to accommodate them. They needed to find a way to show him his behavior was unacceptable in a loving way. But ministering to the boy was farthest from their minds.

The women did not provide for the baby's needs, nor did they take any account of his limitations. How often we push our children beyond their abilities and then blame them for coming up short. The big ones and the little ones and the in the middle children are too often asked to do things for which they are unprepared. Little ones are asked to postpone meal times and sleep time and expected not to get crabby.

The middle school children are expected to make decisions about use of their time, to what they will listen, and what they will watch and read without guidance from adults. Children this age tend to think they can do anything and tend to over commit themselves. They think they should be allowed to make their own decisions, based on the culture and their peers. They need parents to set limits.

Older children are expected to make decisions regarding choice of friends and what they do with their free time when they have no basis for judgment, as when we allow teenage couples to spend too much time alone, leading them into temptation beyond what they can handle.

We must not allow our children to be tempted beyond their ability to resist, God does not do that to us either. Paul wrote, "No temptation has seized you except what is common to man. And God is faithful; He will not let you be tempted beyond what you can bear. But when you are tempted, He will also provide a way out so that you can stand up under it." (1Cor. 10:13)

Had the women in the parking lot accounted for the little boy's limitations, they would have stopped shopping at his lunch time and gotten him lunch, thus providing for his needs. He also needed a nap. Foreseeing this, they could have brought along a favorite cuddly thing or a blanket for him when he got tired.

While the baby was too young to understand complex rules and consequences, he could understand simple rules and the consequences of his choices. I did not see them enter the store or watch while they were shopping, but I suspect from their behavior as they left the store, when the child began to fuss, they fussed back. All three of them were out of control by the time they got to the parking lot.

They probably could have avoided the whole crisis had they told the boy, upon entering the store, what they would be buying, about how long it would take, what they would do for him if he was a good boy the whole time, and the consequences if he wasn't. As they went, had they told him, "Three more things to buy. Two more things to buy, etc.", the time shopping would not have seemed endless.

After accounting for our limitations, our Father lets us know what is expected of us, and the consequences of our behavior. Our Father also allows us freedom of choice. This baby, pushed beyond his limits, had no choice. He could not control himself. He was too tired and hungry and thirsty to make any kind of decision. The time for his decision-making was as they entered the store and while they were shopping. But he apparently was given no decision. It was assumed he would be quiet and docile for as long as his mother and grandmother wanted to shop. Because he could not control himself, he needed his mother and grandmother to be in control of themselves.

Finally, we trust our Father because he keeps His word. When He says He will give us something, He does. When He says we will be disciplined, we are. These women threatened to hit the child, but didn't. They threatened to leave the child, but didn't. Perhaps they said those things because they thought they would shock the little boy into obeying or because they wanted to do those things, whether they were going to actually do them or not.

I do not envy the job those women have in raising that child because of their behavior. There is nothing on which the baby can base trust of his mother or grandmother.

Without trust in their unconditional, unselfish love, he will resent or at least suspect whatever they ask of him. There will be no reason for him to assume that what they ask is for this own good or that they will help him if what they have asked is too hard for him alone. They are building a relationship based on fear. Fear breeds resentment. In addition, one day that boy will be a young man and they will no longer be able to rule him with fear.

In contrast, our relationship with our Father is to be based on trust. He has proven over and over that He has our best interest at heart because He loves us unconditionally and unselfishly. We can try to obey Him, knowing that if we fall short, He will be there to make up the difference and will be quick to forgive. The key is that we want to obey Him because we love Him and we love Him because we can trust Him in all things.

It's easy to trust and love and obey a perfect parent, but none of us is perfect. We will fall short as parents, even as our children will fall short. Even as we, from time to time, rebel against God, our children will rebel against us. We can learn from and model our Father in our parenting, but at times, we will be selfish or prideful or impatient. What are we to do? How can we build relationships with our children based on trust, as our Father has built with us?

We are to do the same thing with our children as we children of God do with our Father, confess and repent. When we ask the Holy Spirit to reveal our shortcomings, and He does, God is quick to forgive when we repent. When we make mistakes in parenting and confess to our children, if our relationship has been built on trust, they will also forgive. We must also be quick to forgive them. When the relationship begins with trust, the children will learn to trust their parents even more when the parents confess their parenting shortcomings. The children will know the parent does not see himself as perfect, nor does he expect perfection. They will know the parent has their best interests at heart, because the parent is willing to confess when he is wrong

Thankfully, when we remember how God parents us, we will make many fewer mistakes in parenting our children. Following these simple principles, our children will take joy in having parents who follow God, just as we can all have joy in knowing we are children of the only Perfect Parent.

Chapter 1 BUILDING TRUST
STUDY PAGE

There are two lessons to be learned from Chapter 1:

LESSON 1: Living as God's child makes us different.

LESSN 2: Trust is earned and learned and leads to obedience with a grateful heart

LESSON 1: Living as God's child makes us different.

APPLICATION: We learn first of all from imitation. What aspect of your life do you not want others, especially your children, to imitate? In what ways do you reflect God's character that you hope your children will imitate?

BIBLE STUDY: List the fruits of the Spirit in Gal. 5:22. How is the person who shows these fruits different from society?

LESSON 2: Trust is earned and learned and leads to obedience with a grateful heart

APPLICATION: Remember a time you trusted God and He proved trustworthy.

BIBLE STUDY: Find one of God's commandments that, on the surface, seems to be for the benefit of someone else, but turns out to be for our own good.

Chapter 2 IN HIS IMAGE
STUDY PAGE

There are 2 lessons in Chapter 2.
LESSON 1: There are ways we are not like God
LESSON 2: With His help we can strive to be like God

APPLICATION: Understanding how far above and beyond us God is should humble us, not only before God, but also before others. In the coming week, keep track of when you have worried about something over which you had little or no control.

BIBLE STUDY: Read Rom. 1:20. Why is no one without excuse of knowing God exists? If no one is without excuse, why do so many people deny the existence of God?

LESSON 2 With His help there are ways we can strive to be like God
APPLICATION: Make a list of the things you do for your family, the roles you have, that are the same for the things God does for you.

BIBLE STUDY: Read Jn. 14:16-17, 14:25-26, and 16:7-11. How does Jesus say the will Holy Spirit help us? How has He helped you?

Chapter 3 WE ARE NOT GOD
STUDY PAGE

There are 2 lessons in Chapter 3.
LESSON 1: As parents, we all fall short
LESSON 2: Because God is who He is, He is a perfect parent

LESSON 1: As parents, we all fall short
APPLICATION: Ask the Holy Spirit to reveal to you, and search yourself for ways in which you fall short as a parent.

BIBLE STUDY: Holy men often had rebellious sons. God killed two of Aaron's sons because they did not prepare the fire as they should. (Lev.10:1-2). Read 1Sam. 2:12-15 and 22-34 and 1Sam. 3:12-14. Why does God punish Eli for the evil of his sons? What had Eli done wrong?

Read 1Sam. 8:1-5. As a parent, what did Samuel do wrong? How did it affect the course of history?

LESSON 2: Because God is who He is, He is a perfect parent
God is eternal and immutable
APPLICATION: We all need to change. None of us is Christ-like yet, perfect in faith, in trust and in love. Each morning or night, ask the Lord to show you areas in which you have been blind to your own shortcomings.

BIBLE STUDY: Look up these verses: Ps. 2:10, 71:16, 139:13, Is. 49:1; Jer. 1:5 What is the earliest you can remember God's hand in your life?

God is Omniscient, Omnipresent and Omnipotent
APPLICATION: Pray for something that is impossible without God's help, something that will glorify Him. Keep track of your prayers and when and how God answered them.

BIBLE STUDY: Read Psalm 46. This Psalm as about God's power and presence. What is the effect on you of knowing God is all-powerful, all knowing and ever present? Relate this to Matt. 6:25-34.

Chapter 4 HIS CHARACTER WE STRIVE FOR
STUDY PAGE

We learn 3 lessons in Chapter 4:
1. God will help us in our parenting.
2. Our heart attitudes are reflected in our behavior.
3. Being a child of God and being a parent start and end with love.

LESSON 1: God will help us in our parenting.
APPLICATION: Loving is a heart attitude. Obeying is the physical manifestation of the love. Yet one can obey without love. Discuss why and how people obey without love and, if you can tell the difference.

BIBLE STUDY: Read Is. 1:9-20 and Matt 15:10-20. The so called holy men of Isaiah's time and Pharisees of Jesus' time thought they were obeying the law by sacrificing. Why is God angry with both of them?

LESSON 2: Our heart attitudes are reflected in our behavior
APPLICATION: As you go through your days, stop often and check your heart attitude about what you are doing. Are you thankful God has given you the job you have and the ability to do it?

Nancy C. Gaughan

BIBLE STUDY: Read: Rom. 13:8-10. Of the Ten Commandments, list those that will reflect your love of your neighbor. For each of the Ten Commandments, discuss how keeping it will show your love of God.

LESSON 3: Being a child of God and being a parent start and end with love.
APPLICATION: What are some of the things you do that spring from your love of God, ways others can see God through you.

BIBLE STUDY: Read John, Chapter 14 and 1John. Why is obedience so important?

Chapter 5 THE HATS OUR FATHER WEARS
STUDY PAGE

We learn of two roles in Chapter 5:
ROLE 1: God is Our Creator
ROLE 2: God is Our Teacher

ROLE 1: God is Our Creator
APPLICATION: Be aware of and make a list of all the things you create through the week. Choose one and write about how it felt to create it and how you felt about it after it was finished.

BIBLE STUDY: Read Is. 42:5-7. Why did God create us?

Read: Eph. 4:22-5:8 Specifically, how does a child of God behave?

ROLE 2: God Is Our Teacher
APPLICATION: List the three most important things God has taught you about Himself or about how to live.

1.

2.

3.

BIBLE STUDY: Read Titus 2. Finish filling out this chart for every group

Who is to Learn	What They Are to Learn
Old Men	Temperate, Worthy of respect, Self-controlled, Sound in faith, love and in endurance
Older Women	
Younger Women	
Younger Men	
Slaves	

Chapter 6: UNCONDITONAL LOVE
STUDY PAGE

One lesson: Just as we know our father loves us unconditionally, our children are to know that we love them unconditionally.

APPLICATION: Write down how knowing that God loves you unconditionally has affected your life.

BIBLE STUDY: The book of Hosea is a picture of God's love for his unfaithful people. Read Hosea. Describe what happens in Hosea in your own words. How does it reassure you?

Father Chapter 7 UNSELFISH LOVE
STUDY PAGE

There are 4 lessons in Chapter 7.
LESSON 1: Loving unselfishly is not natural
LESSON 2: The ability to love unselfishly is a gift from God
LESSON 3: God loves us unselfishly
LESSON 4: With the help of the Holy Spirit, we can love unselfishly

LESSON 1: Loving unselfishly is not natural
APPLICATION: Give an example of selfish love you have seen in others or yourself, not necessarily between parent and child.

BIBLE STUDY: Read: Gen. 25:27-28. What were the effects of Isaac's selfish love for Esau on Rebecca?

On Jacob?

On Esau?

LESSON 2: The ability to love unselfishly is a gift from God
APPLICATION: Think of a person whom you have needed God's love to love. Example: When I am angry with my husband, I ask God to help me love him right then with His love.

BIBLE STUDY: in 1John, John exhorts us repeatedly to love our brothers (and sisters), fellow children of God. Read 1Jn. 4:19-20. How does God loving us enable us to love others?

LESSON 3: God loves us unselfishly
APPLICATION: What evidence do you have in your own life to show that God loves you? Be a witness to His love.

BIBLE STUDY: Discuss the parallel between the Israelite exodus from Egypt (Ex. 12-13:6) and Christ' death on the cross. Who was saved? Saved from what? What lasting effect is the sacrifice to have on God's children?

Lesson 4: With the help of the Holy Spirit, we can love unselfishly
APPLICATION 1: For many reasons we tune people out while they are talking. Focus on giving each person talking to you this week your full, undivided attention. List the people with whom you failed. Is there a pattern? What distracted you?

APPLICATION 2: To remind yourself that God is always listening, keep track of your prayers that God has answered.

BIBLE STUDY: With our children, it is often enough to just listen, but with God's word, our listening is to provoke us to action. Read James 1:19-25. To what kinds of actions should our hearing God's word inspire us? Read 1Jn. 3:1. How will we be different if we reflect our God?

Chapter 8 PROVIDING FOR NEEDS
STUDY PAGE

In this chapter we learn God provides our four basic needs:
LESSON 1: God provides for our emotional needs
LESSON 2: God provides for our spiritual needs
LESSON 3: God provides knowledge, wisdom and understanding
LESSON 4: God provides for our physical needs

LESSON 1: God provides for our emotional needs
APPLICATION: It is often harder to forgive ourselves than to accept God's forgiveness. Describe how God's forgiveness enabled you to forgive either yourself or someone else.

BIBLE STUDY: We can do all the right things and still fail. How? Read Rev. 2:2-4 How is this a summation of Jesus' rebuke of the Pharisees in Matt. 23:11-23?

LESSON 2. God provides for our spiritual needs
APPLICATION: Describe the things you do to reach God and the ways God reaches you.

BIBLE STUDY: Read Ps. 98-101 Write your own psalm to the Lord.

Lesson 3: God provides knowledge, wisdom and understanding
APPLICATION: Jesus said that it is easier for a camel to pass through the eye of a needle than for a rich man to enter into heaven because having riches tends to turn people hearts away from the Lord. Explain why the same thing can be said of the highly educated person. Why are colleges and universities the most antagonistic places to God, especially to Christianity?

Lesson 3: God provides knowledge, wisdom and understanding
BIBLE STUDY: The effect of our wisdom and understanding is to be apparent to others. Read Prov. 2. How does Solomon say our wisdom will be manifest and how will we benefit from wisdom?

Lesson 4: God provides for our physical needs
APPLICATION: What is the one physical thing God has given you that you treasure most?

BIBLE STUDY: God commands us to take care of the poor in our land. Read Deut. 24:10-22. These are practical ways the people of Biblical times could take care of the poor, but they do not fit in our society today. Deut. 15:11 is the principal God is making. How can we do better? What would be the effect on our country if every professed Christian tithed and every church gave a tithe of its donations to private institutions that serve the poor?

Chapter 9 ACCOUNTING FOR LIMITATIONS
STUDY PAGE

There are three lessons in Chapter 9:
1. God has taken our limitations into account
2. God knows we cannot live up to His standards without His help
3. God is patient and forgiving as we learn and grow

Lesson 1: God has taken our limitations into account
APPLICATION: Often we set standards for ourselves that are higher than those God has set for us. We set standards higher than God's by not recognizing our need or the availability for help from the people God's put into our lives. What situations are you most likely to try to push through on your own, not seeking help from other people?

BIBLE STUDY: God's standard for us has never changed. Jesus said the two great commandments we are to love God with all our heart, mind, soul and strength (Deut. 6:5, Matt. 22:37) and to love our neighbors as ourselves. (Lev. 19:18, Matt. 22:39) Paul said all the commandments boiled down to these two. (Rom. 13:9) Read Lev. 19: 1-18 and describe the relationship between these two commandments and the commandments in these verses.

Lesson 2: We cannot live up to God's standards without His help
APPLICATION: Look into your life. What human helpers has God sent to you? How did you recognize them?

BIBLE STUDY: The Holy Spirit has many functions. The Spirit convicts us of for sin, righteousness and judgment. (John 16:7-8) He produces the fruits of the Spirit.(Gal. 5:22-23). He also gives each of us spiritual gifts. Read 1Cor. 12. Which gifts has He given you and how can you, do you use your gifts in the body of your local church and the greater church throughout the world?

Lesson 3: God is patient and forgiving as we learn and grow
APPLICATION: List the activities that clutter your life, activities that keep you too busy for time with God, your family, or a friend. (They may be very worthwhile activities.)

APPLICATION: Find in your past someone whom you have had trouble forgiving. Pray first for God to enable you to forgive that person, then pray for that person.

BIBLE STUDY: It is hope and faith in the future that enables us to wait. Read Ps. 37. What is David certain the Lord will do? What advice does he have for us?

BIBLE STUDY: Read Matt. 18:21-35. In these verses, Jesus makes clear how this, "forgive and you will be forgiven" works. Describe what happens here and the consequence of not forgiving.

Chapter 10 COMMUNICATING INSTRUCTIONS AND CONSEQUENCES STUDY PAGE

There are 4 lessons in Chapter 10
Lesson 1: God first establishes His love and trustworthiness
Lesson 2: God tell us the consequences when He tell us the instructions
Lesson 3: God's can tell us what to do because He is God
Lesson 4: We must ask and trust God to enable us to obey

Lesson 1: God first establishes His love and trustworthiness
APPLICATION: 1. When have you trusted God that He proved faithful?

When have you an opportunity to prove yourself trustworthy?

BIBLE STUDY: Read through the "remember" references in the epistles. (Rom 8, 12-15; 1 Cor. 10:1-33, 15:2-34; Gal 3-6; Eph. all; Phil. 2:5-16, 3-4; Col. 2-4; Titus 3:1-11; Heb. all; 1Pet. all, 2Pet 1:1-21, 3:11-18, 1Jn. all.) Choose the one that would best convince you that God is trustworthy and loves you.

Lesson 2: God tells us the consequences when He tell us the instructions

APPLICATION: We make cause and consequence decisions all the time, like whether to speed when we are in a hurry. We weigh the cost of a ticket and the probability of getting away with it with the need to get some place. How does knowing that God is all knowing and ever present help you to walk in His ways?

BIBLE STUDY: Which of God's commandments is the hardest for you to follow and which brings you the most comfort?

Lesson 3: God's can tell us what to do because He is God
APPLICATION: Every position, parent, spouse, teacher, mechanic, engineer, is a position of trust. What happens in families, in business, and in our country when people betray each others' trust?

BIBLE STUDY: Read Deut. 17:14-20. List the rules God gave the future king. Read 1Kgs. 3:1-2, 7:1-12; 10:1-11:8. How did Solomon betray his people?

Lesson 4: We must trust to enable us to obey
APPLICATION: Forgiveness does not come naturally. Vengeance does. Yet, we are commanded to forgive. (Matt. 6:14-15) How does trusting God enable you to forgive?

BIBLE STUDY: Read: Prov. 17:9 and 19:11. What does it mean to take no offense? What does Solomon say are the benefits of not taking offense?

What is a circumstance you have faced when you did not take offense, but you could have?

Chapter 11 ALLOWING FREEDOM OF CHOICE
STUDY PAGE

There are lessons 6 in lesson 11:
Lesson 1: God has given us freedom to choose to obey or not.
Lesson 2: Our natural inclination is to do it our own way.
Lesson 3: People usually react badly to rebellion in others
Lesson 4: God is not passive, but proactive in letting us choose
Lesson 5: It is appropriate to sometimes intervene
Lesson 6: We need God's wisdom to know when to act or step back

Lesson 1: God has given us freedom to choose to obey or not
APPLICATION: Keep track one day. How many choices to you make? For which of these decisions did you seek God's guidance or refer to what you already know from His word?

BIBLE STUDY: Describe your stance on predestination. Support it with specific verses.

APPLICATION: We fail both in being rebellious ourselves and in reacting badly to the rebellion in our children. What are your particular strengths as a parent?

What are your most glaring shortcomings and how can God help you with them?

Lessons 2-3: People are naturally rebellious and generally react badly to rebellion in others.
BIBLE STUDY: Read 2Sam. 13:1-27. Summarize the plot. Describe David's fault as a parent in vs. 21-23 and vs. 24.

Lesson 4: God is not passive, but proactive in letting us choose
APPLICATION: What choices have you made that affected your whole life? What led you to choose as you did?

BIBLE STUDY: Jesus said that anyone who sins, and that is all of us, is a slave to sin. (Jn. 8:34) And Paul wrote in Rom. 7:14-19 we are all slaves to sin because of our natural inclination. Yet, Paul exhorts us to be holy. Read Eph. 4:17-24, 5:8-17, 6:10-18. How can we, inherently sinful people live God's way?

Lesson 5: It is appropriate to sometimes intervene
APPLICATION: Describe a time God intervened in your life to keep you from a bad decision or keep you from the consequence of a bad decision.

Lesson 5: It is appropriate to sometimes intervene
BIBLE STUDY: Read: Rom. 5:6-10. How has knowing this changed your life and your relationships?

Lesson 6: We need God's wisdom to know when to act or step back
APPLICATION: Describe a time when you intervened when you shouldn't have.

Describe a time when you did not intervene when you should have.

BIBLE STUDY: Our tasks are not unlike David's or Solomon's. We must make rules and stand by them. We must protect and defend our people. We must know when to intervene and when to step back. Read: Job 28:12-24 and 1Kgs. 3:5-11. What are the implications for your life?

Chapter 13 STAYING IN CONTROL
STUDY PAGE

There are 3 lessons in Chapter 13
Lesson 1: Peace comes from trusting God
Lesson 2: Getting out of control comes from unrealistic expectations
Lesson 3: If we focus on God we can stay in control

Lesson 1: Peace comes from trusting God
APPLICATION: Describe a time you panicked when, had you trusted God, you would have stayed calm.

BIBLE STUDY: Describe what happens in Ex. 14:9-31. Based on this experience, explain the Israelites' reaction in Num. 13:1-14:9

Lesson 2: Getting out of control comes from unrealistic expectations
APPLICATION: Describe how you felt when someone was very angry with you.

BIBLE STUDY: Read 1Sam. 14:1-45. Saul's anger led him to force an oath on his men. What was the oath? Why was it foolish? How did it lead his son and his men to defy him?

Lesson 3: If we focus on God, we can stay in control
APPLICATION: Describe what you will do to stay in control when
things suddenly go wrong and you start to get very angry.

BIBLE STUDY: READ Judges 14:10-15:15. Does knowing that
God could use Samson's self righteous anger to hurt the Philistines
affect how you feel about Samson?

BIBLE STUDY: READ Deut. 9:1-21. What is the purpose of Moses
reminding the Israelites of their sins and what the Lord has done
and is going to do for them? How did Moses stave off Gods wrath?
What does this teach you about interceding for your children, even
when you are as angry as Moses must have been?

Chapter 14 THE PERFECT PARENT
STUDY PAGE

There is 1 lesson in Lesson 14: God is the perfect parent
APPLICATION: What parts of this study will be the most difficult
for you to put into practice?

How will you accomplish the change?

BIBLE STUDY: Write a description of your Father in Heaven, based
solely on Matt. 5-7. How do you compare?

SCRIPTURAL REFERENCES

All from New American Standard Bible (NASB)

Chapter 1.
Prov. 22:6
Isa. 55:8
Gal. 5:22-23
Rom. 1:20
1Jn. 4:8
Jn. 15:11
1Pet. 3:20
Lk. 6:35
Ps. 100:5
2Th. 3:3
Matt. 11:29
Is. 53:7

Chapter 2.
Gen. 1:27
Prov. 22:6
Deut. 10:12-13
1Cor. 7:35
Jn. 14:15
Prov. 3:12
Eph. 6:13-18

Chapter 3.
Heb. 13:8
Jn. 1:1

Ps. 90:2
Gen. 21:33
Deut. 33:37
Is. 26:4
1Tim. 1:17
Jn. 3:16
Ps. 2:10
Ps. 71:16
Ps. 139:13
Is. 49:1
Jer. 1:5
Mal. 3:6
James 1:17
Matt. 7:24-26
Ps. 51:5
Rom. 7:18
Rom. 8:29
Phil. 3:10
1Jn. 4:17
Eph. 4:22-24
Matt. 5:48
Job 21:22
Prov. 2:6
Deut. 31:6, 31:8
Josh. 1:5
Ps. 46:1

Heb. 1:14
Mark 1:8
Jn. 14:16
Acts 2:38
Gen. 1, 2
Ex. 14:13-30
Josh. 4:23-24
Josh. 10:12-13
James 1:5
Rom. 8:28
Is. 45:22
Matt. 6:35
1Pet. 4:11
Matt. 6:35
1Pet. 4:11
Lev. 10:1-2
1Sam. 2:2-15
1Sam. 2:22-34
1Sam. 3:12—14
1Sam. 8:1-5
Ps. 2:10
Ps. 71:16
Ps. 139: 13
Is. 49:1
Jer. 1:5
Ps. 46
Matt. 6:25-34

Eph. 4:32
Ps. 77:13
Ps. 99:3
Is. 6:3
Heb. 4:15
Ps. 143:2
Rom. 3:23
Jn. 1:8
Lev. 20:26
Lev. 21:8
1Pet. 1:15-16
Lev. 20:26
Lev. 21:8
1Jn. 1:9
Gal. 5:19-21
Matt. 15:18
Lk. 6:37
Ps. 51:10
1Jn. 3:6
Jn. 8:34
1Cor. 10:13
Mk. 12:30-21
Is. 1:9-20
Matt. 15:10-12
Rom. 13:8-10
Jn. 14
1Jn. All

Chapter 4.

Rom. 8:29
Jn. 14:15-17
Gal. 5:22-23
Matt. 5:44-47
Lk. 6:27-31
Ps. 145:9
2Ths. 1:6
Prov. 3:12

Chapter 5.

Deut. 32:26
Ps. 139: 13
Ps. 22:10
Gen. 1:27
Gen. 2:7
Gen. 1:31
Jer. 16:21
Ex. 1:15

Is. 48:17
Ps. 25:8-9
Ps. 25: 8-9
Prov. 1:1-6
1Cor. 7:35
Lk. 16:15
Rev. 3:17
Jn. 3:17
Deut. 4:9
Deut. 11:19
1Pet. 1:8-9
Is. 42:5-7
Eph. 4:22-29
Titus 2

Chapter 6.

Ps.100:5
Ps.136
Heb.11:8-10
Gen. 12:2
Gen. 12:17
Gen. 13:5-12
Lk. 15:11-24
Lk. 15:11-13
Lk. 15:14-19
Pro. 22:6
Lk. 15:20
Matt. 18 21-22
Judges 2:11
Judges 3:7
Judges 3:12
Judges 4:1
Judges 6:1
Judges 10:6
Judges 13:1
Rom. 8:38-39

Chapter 7.

Jn. 3:16
2Sam. 11:1o-4
Gen. 37:3
Gen. 35: 5-11
Lk. 6:32
1Thes. 4:9
1Cor. 13:4-7
Acts 9:13-28
2Cor. 11:23-30
Phil. 1:23-24
Rom. 9:1-5
Rom. 9:3-4
Job 1:3
Job 1:4
Job 1:5
Gal. 3:20
Jn. 3:16
Gal. 2:16
Is. 1:11
Jer. 6:20
Ps. 141:2
Jer. 29:12-13
Ps. 34:17
Prov. 15:29
Ps. 69:33
Job 22:27
Is 65:24
Jer. 29:11-12
Mal. 7:7
Gen. 25:27-28
1Jn. 4:19-20
Ex. 12:13:6
James 1:19-25
1Jn. 3:1

Chapter 8.

Ps 19:1
2Tim. 3:16
Job 12:13
Prov. 2:6
James 1:5
Eccl. 2:26
Job 15:8
Isa. 29:14
Matt. 6:31-33
Matt. 7:9-11
Ex. 16:1-17:6
Deut. 8:3-4
Deut. 7:12-26
Deut. 28:1-14
Ex. 31:3
Ex. 20:18-19
Rev. 2:2-4
Matt. 23:11-23
Ps. 98-101
Prov. 2
Deut. 24: 16-22

Chapter 9.

Rom. 2:23
Prov. 22:6
1Cor. 10:13
1Pet. 2:21-22
Deut. 6:5
Matt. 22:37
Lev. 19:18
Matt. 22:39
Rom. 3:23
Jer. 4:22
1Jn. 1:8
Lev. 4:2-4
Lev. 5:15

Eph. 1:4
Isa. 6:5
Jer. 3:34
1Jn. 1:9
Matt. 26:28
Rom. 3:21-22
Rom. 7:19-20
Lk. 11:13
Jn. 14:16-17
Jn. 16:8
1Sam 8:3
Deut. 10:13
Gen. 3:12-13
Gen. 14-19
1Jn. 1:9
Rom. 2:4
Rom. 9:22
1Tim. 1:16
2Pet. 3:9
Phil. 1:6
Matt. 12
Mark 2-3
Lk. 6:13-7:4
Matt. 8:27
Matt. 21:20
Matt. 22:22
Mark 6:51
Mark 10:24-26
Mark 8:31-32
James 1:5
1Jn. 1:9
Deut. 6:5
Matt. 12:37
Lev. 1918
Matt. 22:39
Rom. 13:9
Lev. 19:1-18

Jn. 16:7-8
Gal. 5:22-23
1Cor. 12
Ps.37

Chapter 10.
Isa. 2:3
Acts 2:14-40
Acts 3:12-26
Acts 7:1-53
Acts 13:14-42
Rom. 8:12-15
1Cor. 10:1-33
1Cor. 15:2-34
Gal 3-6
Eph. All
Phil. 2: 5-16
Phil. 3 4
Col. 2o-4
Titus 3:1-11
Heb. All
1Pet. All
2Pet. 1:21
1Jn. All
Gen. 2:16-17
Matt. 6:14:15
Lev. 11:44-45
Lev 18: 2, 4-6
Lev. 21:30
Lev. 19: 3-4
Lev. 10
Lev. 14
Lev. 16
Lev. 18
Lev. 25
Lev. 28
Lev. 30-32

Lev. 34
Lev. 36
Lev. 37
Lev. 20
Lev. 7
Lev. 24
Lev. 21:12, 15, 23
Lev. 22:2-3
Lev. 8-9
Lev. 16: 30-33
Lev. 23:22, 43
Lev. 24:22
Lev. 25:17, 38,55
Lev. 26: 1-2
Lev. 13: 44-45
Deut. 10:13
Jn. 14:15
Deut. 9:23
Gen. 14:18-20
Matt. 23:23
Lk. 14:42
Mal. 3:8-10
Matt. 26:42
Rom. 8:12-15
1Cor. 10:1-33
1Cor. 15:2-34
Gal. 3-6
Eph. All
Phil. 2:5-16
Phil. 3, 4
Col. 2-4
Deut. 17:14-20
1Kgs. 3:1-2
1Kgs. 7:1-12
1Kgs. 10:1-11:8
Prov. 17:9
Prov. 19:11

Chapter 11.
Gen. 2:16
Gen. 2:17
Deut. 30:19
Judg. 2:11
Judg. 3:7
Judg. 4:1
Judg. 4:1
Judg. 6:1
Judg. 10:6
Judg. 13:1
Judg. 17:6
Judge. 21:25
Rom. 7:14-19
Josh. 1:5
Prov. 3:31
Prov. 5:10
Prov. 16:16
Jonah 1:416
Jonah 2:10
Matt. 23:25
Lk. 11:39
Jonah 4:6
Jonah 4:10-11
Job 12:13
Job. 15:8
2Sam. 13:1-27
Jn. 8:34
Rom 7:14-19
Eph. 4:17-21
Eph. 6:10-18
Rom. 5:6-10
Job. 28:12-24
1Kgs. 3:5-11

Chapter 12.
Neh. 9:8

Gen. 19:1-11
Deut. 29:9-15
Josh. 6:18-20
Josh. 7:1-23
Gen. 13:16
Gen. 22:17
Gen. 15:13
Gen. 13: 15, 17
Gen. 26:4
Matt. 1"1-17
Jn. 14: 1-o4
2Pet. 3:8-9
Gen. 22:17
Gen. 25:20-25
Gen. 15:13
Deut. 28:62-68
Matt. 26:14-16
Matt 26: 47-50
2Pet. 3
1 Chron. 16:7o-36
Isa. 13:1-11

Chapter 13.
Prov. 29:11
Eph. 4:26
Eph. 4:31
Gal. 5:22-23
Lk. 8:22-23
Prov. 6:19
Rom. 8:28
Ps. 25:3
Isa. 13:6o-9
Ex. 14:9-31
Num. 13:1-14:9
1Sam. 14:1-45
Judg. 14:10-15:15
Deut. 9:121

Chapter 14.
Matt. 5:48
Gal. 5:22-23
1Jn. 4:8
Deut. 31:6
Jonah 1:3-2:10
Lk. 19:10
Jn. 3:17
Jn. 3:16
Acts 14:17
1Jn. 4:10
1Cor. 10:13
Matt. 5-7